Shakespeare's Notebook

The Life, Times and Works of

William Shakespeare

Shakespeare's Notebook

The Life, Times and Works of

William Shakespeare

Written and Compiled by

Sophie Collins

The History Press

First published in the United Kingdom in 2026 by
The History Press
97 St. George's Place
Cheltenham
Gloucestershire
GL50 3QB
www.thehistorypress.co.uk

EU Authorised Representative: Easy Access System Europe
Mustamäe tee 50, 10621 Tallinn, Estonia
gpst.request@easproject.com
Printed in Huizhou, Guangdong, China
TT/Feb/2026

2 4 6 8 10 9 7 5 3 1

ISBN: 978 1 83705 150 2

Conceived, designed and produced by
The Bright Press, an imprint of The Quarto Group
1 Triptych Place, London, SE1 9SH, United Kingdom.
T (0)20 7700 6700
www.quarto.com

Design and Image Research: Lindsey Johns

Contents

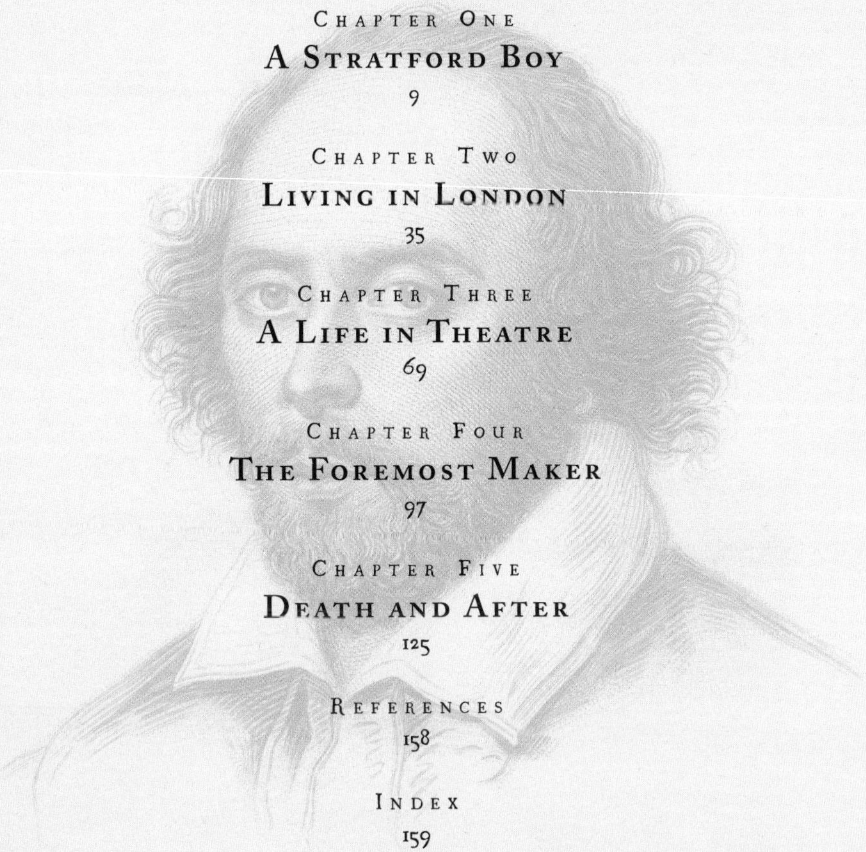

Introduction

Finding Will
William Shakespeare didn't emerge from a vacuum, but his huge legacy, not to mention a four-century remove, makes it hard for us to find him as a real person, surrounded by other people, within the large, complex system of Tudor and Jacobean theatre. To place him where he belongs, in a crowd of his peers, we need to put him into context and repopulate his world.

His background doesn't give us much to go on. He was one of eight children, son of a tradesman, out in the provinces. A career in theatre seemed unlikely, but Christopher Marlowe, equally lauded in his time and with a more dramatic – and shorter – life, was the son of a Canterbury cobbler, so Shakespeare wasn't unique. Neither man started out with useful connections. Somehow (the enduring mystery of those famous 'missing years'), Shakespeare made his way to London and started to write, and to write successfully. From early on, he had the support of a theatre company who needed what he wrote to keep them in business – Tudor theatre was led by a constant need for novelty. Plus, he had the resources of the capital – a mix of people from different social backgrounds; a city's worth of books to borrow, plays to watch and traveller's tales to absorb. The theatre also gave him proximity to the monarch and the court, with the potential for patronage.

The Soul of the Age

Shakespeare seems to have been both workmanlike and flexible, able to turn all these possibilities to his advantage. When the theatres were closed by plague, he wrote profitable poetry; when it was practical to write in collaboration, that's what he did. We know he was a good team player because he stayed with his theatre company for more than 20 years, and when he died, its members seem sincerely to have mourned him. Shakespeare had also picked one of the few professions of his time which enabled a man to move in different social classes relatively easily. By 1601, only a decade after he's heard of in London, *Twelfth Night* became the first of his plays to be performed at court.

We'll find the 'real' Shakespeare in the businessman as well as the artist. As he wrote a stream of masterpieces, he was steadily buying up property, building a fortune against bad luck, aware that success might not last. The early modern age, one of discovery and innovation, of religious flux, constant outbreaks of plague and a restless search after the new, suited him as perhaps no other time would have done, satisfying both his practical and his romantic sides. As we'll find, rather than simply existing there, it was the perfect fit for him, the 'soul of the age'.

Opposite: Painted in 1849 by Sir John Gilbert, *The Plays of William Shakespeare* is a conversation piece made up of some key characters – a raving Lear, a cavorting Falstaff, and Portia and Shylock engaged in a courtroom face-off among them.

Below: The man himself, in a near-contemporary engraving.

Bottom: Shakespeare and his friends enjoying a rather genteel-looking evening at his local, the Mermaid Tavern, in an engraving from 1850.

CHAPTER ONE

A STRATFORD BOY

John Shakespeare

A Rural Yeoman
Shakespeare's father was born into a farming family in the village of Snitterfield in Warwickshire. Most of what we know about him comes from a handful of surviving documents. He was probably born early in the 1530s; by 1552, he had moved a few miles to Stratford, the nearest town.

We can pin the date down because of a mundane entry in the Stratford court ledger for April 1552. It lists John Shakespeare as one of three citizens to be fined for allowing a midden, or dung heap, to accumulate in the street outside his front door. Despite this, he was already doing well, both socially and financially.

A Man on the Rise

Like many men of his time, John Shakespeare worked at multiple jobs. Historians think he could read but probably not write – he 'signed' legal documents with a rough drawing of a pair of compasses. His semi-literacy didn't hold him back, however. He was one of a number of glovers in Stratford at a period when elegant gloves were in-demand accessories for gentlefolk, and strong, plain ones were as necessary to manual workers as a good pair of boots (the compasses of his signature were a key tool in

Below: Gloves like this with elaborately embellished cuffs were essential accessories for Tudor gentry and aristocrats.

Right: Looking towards Stratford from the Clopton Bridge, built by a local landowner in 1492.

Below right: Tudor houses on the outskirts of Stratford – when the town was in a completely rural setting.

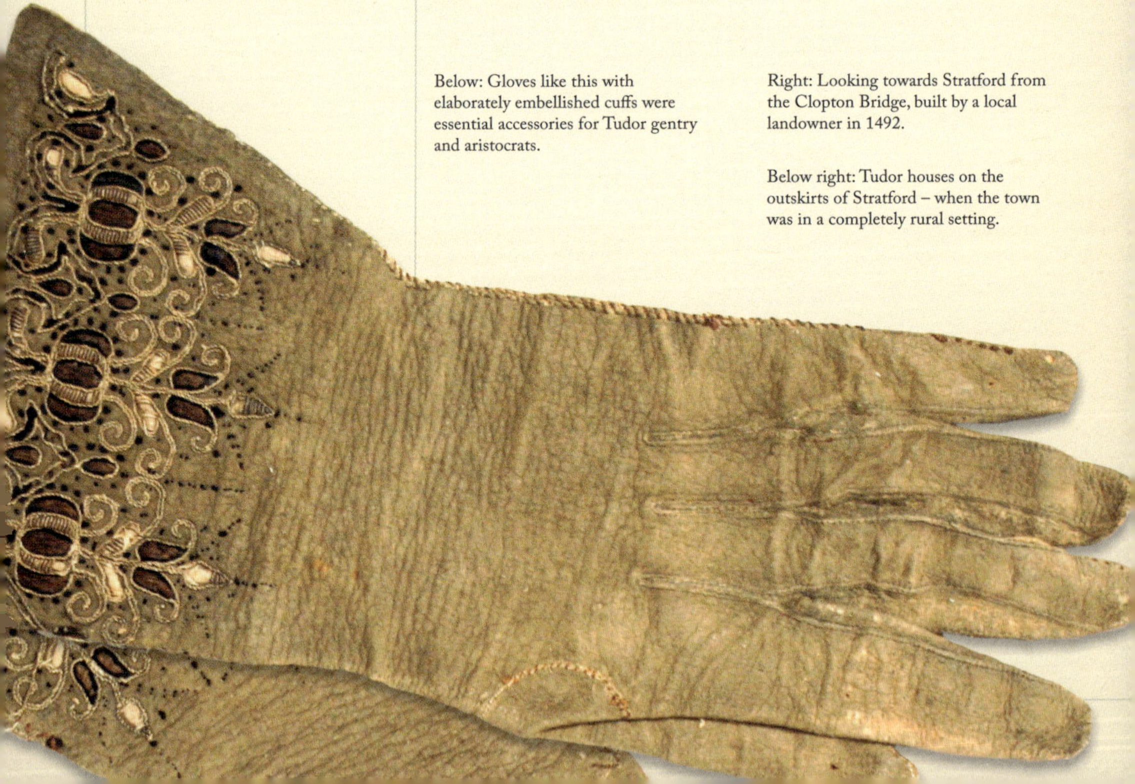

the glover's trade). He seems to have tanned his own leather, too. And on top of this, he dealt in wool – a profitable enterprise, although an illegal one, since he didn't hold the necessary permit. Finally, he acted as an informal money lender. Later in life these last two activities would come back to bite him, but his early years in Stratford were certainly a story of success.

John Shakespeare owned three houses by the late 1550s, including the house in Granary Street, which is widely accepted as William's birthplace. As well as his businesses, he held a succession of civic positions – by 1566 he was an alderman, and finally, in 1568, he was appointed bailiff, a post equivalent to a town's mayor.

'To business that we love we rise betimes And go to't with delight.'

—*Antony and Cleopatra*, Act IV, Scene IV

Mary Arden

The Advantageous Match
When John Shakespeare chose a wife in 1557, he picked Mary, youngest of eight daughters of Robert Arden, the well-off tenant farmer from whom his own father rented land. Effectively, he married the boss's daughter.

Robert owned both the farmland in Snitterfield, which he rented out, and around 70 acres in Wilmcote, which he farmed himself. He died a year before John and Mary's marriage, having appointed Mary as his executrix, which means that she was possibly literate, although, like her husband-to-be, she signed documents with a mark – in her case a horse – rather than a signature. She benefitted personally from her father's will; he left her both cash and the farm, Asbyes, in Wilmcote, and this inheritance will have helped the young couple's rise to prosperity in the late 1550s and '60s.

A Quiet Life

What was Mary like? The short answer is, we can't really know – we don't have even the sparse civic footprint that allows us to piece together her husband's jigsaw. This isn't unusual: generally,

'That a woman conceived me, I thank her; that she brought me up, I likewise give her most humble thanks.'

—*Much Ado About Nothing*, Act 1, Scene 1

only aristocratic women, with both education and the leisure to make use of it, left their mark on Elizabethan society. The wife of a small-town businessman would have kept busy running her household, managing her servants, having a lot of children and dealing with day-to-day life, which involved, by today's standards, plenty of heavy manual work.

Mary was born around 1537 – we don't have an exact date – and she gave birth to eight children. The oldest two daughters died in infancy; William, born in 1564, was the first to survive. He, three brothers and one sister lived to adulthood, and another daughter died aged just seven. This kind of headcount wasn't very unusual; around 14 per cent of children in Elizabeth's reign died before they were a year old, and the risk of dying in childbirth was also high. Mary not only raised a largeish family but also lived to be old. She died, aged around 71, in 1608.

Below: Mary Arden's birthplace at Wilmcote still stands today. Built in around 1513 by her father, Robert, it's where she spent her childhood.

Stratford in 1564

SMALL-TOWN LIFE

In the year William Shakespeare was born, Stratford was a thriving market town, prettily situated on the River Avon, with an estimated population of around 2,000. During his brief reign, Edward VI had 'incorporated' the town – that is, decreed that it would be run by an appointed group, the corporation; he also, in 1553, founded a grammar school there.

With a civic body to manage its interests, Stratford had reached a certain standing by the mid-16th century. Crossing the river coming to and from town was no longer dependent, as in medieval times, on small ferries or, when the Avon was low, on a ford. Instead, people could use the Clopton Bridge, which still survives: a handsome stone structure built in 1492. The use of much of the surrounding land had shifted over the 15th and early 16th centuries from arable crops to sheep farming, the better to serve a booming wool trade.

The Church of the Holy Trinity, built in Saxon times, had been remodelled to suit the needs of the community's growing congregation – and disfigured, like so many others, during Henry VIII's Reformation, during which most of its decorative carvings were smashed.

An Unwelcome Visitor

If this picture of a rural town sounds appealing, Stratford also, like every smallish parochial community, had its fair share of problems. The biggest threat, though, was sickness – throughout the Tudor period it suffered from recurrent outbreaks of plague; 1564 was a particularly bad year. The first infections were identified in July, and by December the disease had killed more than 200 people before it loosened its grip at the turn of the year. Having lost their first two daughters, the Shakespeares must have feared for their baby son, just three months old, but in this year at least, no-one in their family seems to have been affected.

Opposite left: The child king Edward VI, famous both for his love of learning and his ardent Protestantism.

Opposite right: Stratford's new bridge made travel, and thus trade, in and out of the town much easier.

Below left: A woodcut from 1532, showing the grim effects of a sudden outbreak of plague.

Below: Corpse bearers and gravediggers were hired – and relatively well paid – by the town's corporation. Nonetheless, they were unpopular jobs.

'Physic himself must fade
All things to end are made,
The plague full swift goes by;
I am sick, I must die.
~ Lord, have mercy on us!'

—Thomas Nashe, 'A Litany in Time of Plague', 1600

Life Under Elizabeth I

The Wider World
Elizabeth I was 25 when she acceded to the throne in November 1558, after a hectic decade which had seen the child king Edward VI succeeding his father Henry VIII, then himself being succeeded by Queen Mary.

Edward and Mary's brief reigns had been turbulent and the new queen's subjects probably hoped that she would bring some stability. She was intelligent, tough and skilled at PR, while her youthful beauty added glamour to her image. 'Her mind is no womanly weakness [sic] and her perseverance is equal to that of a man', her tutor, Roger Ascham, had written in 1548, when she was just 15.

Right: Queen Elizabeth in full state array; an engraving from a contemporary painting, showing her with all the symbols of her rule – orb, sceptre and rich (and cumbersome) dress.

Opposite: Robert Dudley, Earl of Leicester, painted in about 1560. A friend of Elizabeth's from childhood, he hoped to marry her. The magnificent festivities in 1575 at Kenilworth, centre, may have been intended to woo her; if so, they were unsuccessful.

'A mayden Queene, that shone as Titans ray,
In glistring gold, and peerelesse pretious stone
Yet her bright blazing beautie did assay
To dim the brightnesse of her glorious throne...'

—Edmund Spenser flatters an ageing Elizabeth, *The Faerie Queene*, 1590

Regal Public Relations

Elizabeth made extensive summer 'progresses' around the country – tours during which she stayed in the great houses of her aristocracy, while making regular appearances in public.

What would John Shakespeare and his family have felt about her? There's a theory that he had Catholic leanings which wouldn't have made him enthusiastic, but like everyone else he must have been curious to see her in the flesh. In 1575, after nearly two decades on the throne, Elizabeth made a spectacular visit to Warwickshire during a summer progress. She stayed at the refurbished Kenilworth Castle, seat of her court favourite, Robert Dudley, Earl of Leicester. Her longest visit, it cleaned Dudley out financially; it lasted 17 days, during which there were fireworks, pageants and theatricals. Kenilworth is close to Stratford, and many local families went along to see the show and catch a glimpse of the monarch. If 11-year-old William Shakespeare was there, perhaps it lit the performing fire in him, as well as offering a look at a monarch he would have much more to do with in future.

Religion in Everyday Life

An Uneasy Truce

A modern reader might assume that England's religious position stabilised during the age of Elizabeth, after the rules of first, fervently Protestant Edward, then equally fervently Catholic Mary. And although some aspects remained vexed through her reign, she got off to a relatively moderate start.

Today, when few people are shocked by either agnosticism or atheism, it's hard to grasp how central to everything faith was in Shakespeare's time. Almost everyone was religious. Life was precarious; most believed strongly in an afterlife, including heaven and hell. While you were still alive, adherence to the wrong faith could get you imprisoned or, at especially tense moments, even killed.

With Elizabeth, Protestantism once again became the norm. In 1558 she passed the Acts of Recusancy, compelling everyone to attend church services and worship according to the Church of England. Her arrival was unwelcome to Catholic-leaning subjects, and the country waited with bated breath to see who she would marry (a Catholic or Catholic-sympathising husband might set the merry-go-round going again). Ultimately, she stuck to her status as the Virgin Queen – but early in her reign the speculation was endless.

*'Now, God be praised, that to believing souls
Gives light in darkness, comfort in despair!'*

—*Henry VI*, Part 2, Act 2, Scene I

Mary Queen of Scots
1542-1567

A Mysterious Document

Some scholars think that John Shakespeare held Catholic beliefs, but although he was fined for recusancy, he claimed that he'd failed to attend the – obligatory – church services because he was avoiding people to whom he owed money. A more intriguing piece of evidence was a document allegedly found by builders in the rafters of the Shakespeare home in the mid-18th century. It was a pamphlet, dating to John's time, annotated and containing strongly Catholic views. It quickly passed into Shakespearean legend although – naturally – it went missing soon after discovery. Is the story apocryphal? We can't know; it left a lingering belief, though, that William Shakespeare was brought up in a Catholic-leaning home.

Opposite: The devoutly Catholic Mary Queen of Scots was a long-term threat to Elizabeth I. Constant plots to put her on the throne would ultimately lead to her execution.

Above: Strong religious faith, practised both publicly and in private, was the assumed norm in Tudor England.

Childhood

Work and Play
Childhood in Tudor times was concertinaed: overall life expectancy was shorter, and children were in training for adulthood from a very young age. Much of a parent's role consisted of getting their offspring to a competent independence as fast as possible.

Given the high rate of infant mortality, babies were baptised within a day or two of birth – no-one wanted their child to die outside the Church. The circumstances in which the Shakespeare children spent baby- and toddlerhood would seem very bare to us – uncomfortable, chilly houses where the sparse furniture had plenty of sharp corners. If your parents were poor, you might be put to work while you were still very young indeed; in the country, even a five-year-old might be sent to scare crows away from a crop, for example. But in better-off families like Shakespeare's, small children would be fed, clothed (in unisex dresses until they were about six, when the boys were 'breeched') and kept as safe as was possible in a perilous world.

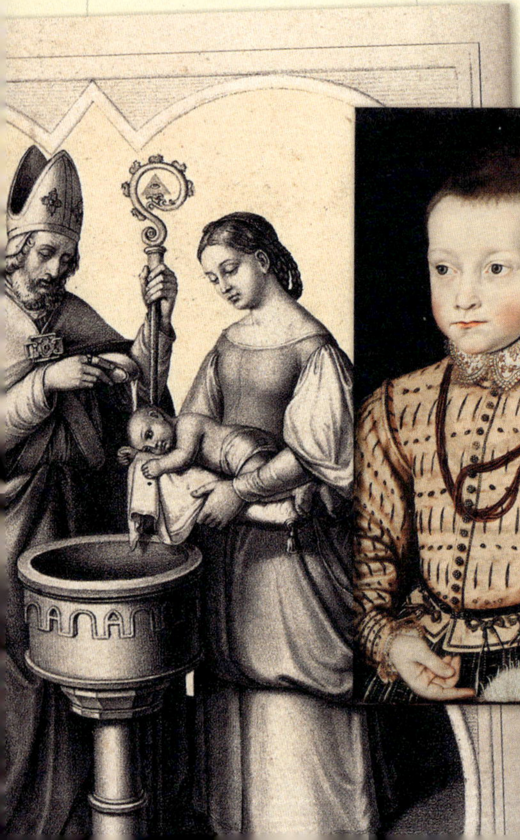

'Honour thy father and thy mother'

Obedience was important and once children were out of toddlerhood, discipline could be harsh. Keeping your children in line was a parental duty – it didn't mean that you loved them any less, but it did indicate the importance of getting them ready for life's challenges. Before they were dispatched to work or school, though, Tudor children played like the children of any time – ballgames were perennially popular, and toys might be bought, or improvised from the abundance of natural materials out of doors: dolls ('poppets'), rattles, hoops, spinning tops and hobby horses make regular appearances in contemporary prints. More luxuriously, wood- and metalworkers sold child-sized novelties – tiny chairs or pewter ewers – alongside their regular goods.

'To you your father should be as a god,
One that composed your beauties, yea, and one
To whom you are but as a form in wax...'

—*A Midsummer Night's Dream*, Act 1, Scene 1

Opposite left: Babies were baptised shortly after birth to ensure they were eligible to enter heaven should the worst happen.

Opposite right: An aristocratic Tudor family, dressed like little adults, as was the custom of the time.

Above: Dutch painter Pieter Bruegel's masterpiece, *Children's Games*, painted in 1560, is a wonderful encyclopedic reference to contemporary play. It depicts over 80 games, from hide and seek to knucklebones.

Shakespeare's Schooling

EARLY LEARNING

Between the ages of four and six, boys – and a few girls – from families with aspirations might attend a 'petty' school, where they would be taught to read and possibly (though not invariably) to write.

Few parents had enough free time to teach their children the basics at home, while extensive private education from tutors was reserved for the rich and aristocratic. Shakespeare was born into an ambitious generation, however – his father had bettered himself socially and probably wanted his children to do the same.

When Henry VIII dissolved the monasteries, he declared that one of his ambitions for some of the riches grabbed was to reinvest them in the education of an elite new generation of Englishmen. Edward VI had gone on to found or modernise a number of grammar schools, including the one in Stratford, as well as publishing the *Book of Common Prayer* in 1549 – the first in English rather than Latin. This included the catechism, a simple question-and-answer routine, setting out the basics of Christian faith and duty.

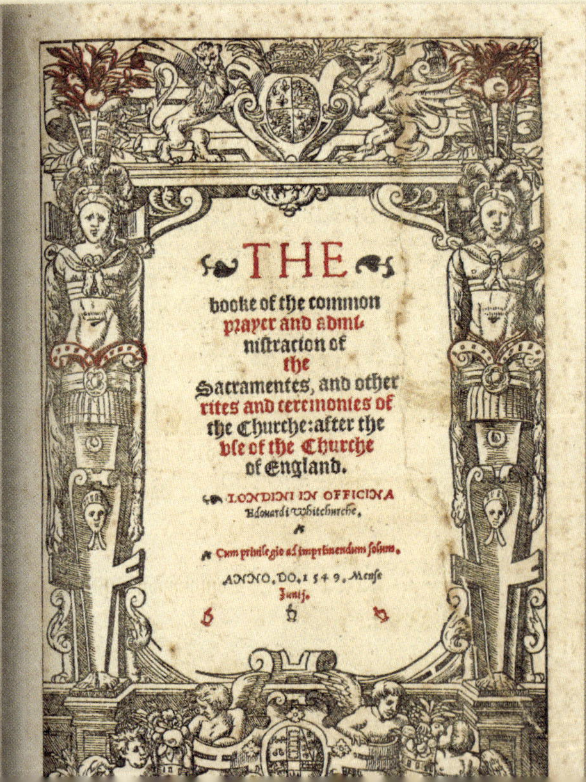

'Some books are to be tasted, others to be swallowed, and some few to be chewed and digested...'

—Francis Bacon, *Of Studies*, 1597

Petty schools were old-style, but they were the first step to an education. Shakespeare seems to have picked up an impressive secondary education at Stratford's grammar school, but a petty school is probably where it all began.

Early Learning

The petty school was usually held in a private house, with just a small number of children. The class would be taught to recite the catechism and learn the alphabet using a hornbook – a flat paddle of wood onto which was pasted a sheet of letters, protected by a thin sheet of transparent horn. Depending on how long the child spent at the school and the quality of teaching, by the time they left, they might still be laboriously spelling out syllables, or be able to read and write fluently. Leaving the petty school saw the end of many children's education.

Opposite: The title page of the *Book of Common Prayer*, the first in English rather than Latin, sponsored by Edward VI and printed in 1549.

Below left: The master hears the lesson from one pupil in a Tudor schoolroom; others sit waiting their turn – apart from the one who has fallen asleep on his bench.

Below: A well-worn hornbook, sturdy enough to withstand everyday accidents and constant use.

A Classical Education

HARD STUDY
One of the advantages of John Shakespeare's civic role on the town council was that William was given his grammar school education for free. Once there, the schedule sounds gruelling: attendance was six days a week, between 6am (7am in winter) and around 5pm.

A boy would begin grammar school aged about seven and leave when he was 14 (those who could afford even more education might then head off to Oxford or Cambridge, the only two universities in England at the time). Sunday was his only day off, although church attendance would have ensured that he didn't get a lot of leisure time. Given this, Shakespeare's description, in *As You Like It,* of the 'whining' schoolboy's unwilling creep to school is understandable. William would have been creeping up the road to Stratford's Guildhall, which housed the King's New School.

A Full Curriculum

Once there, the boys were under the tuition of a master who earned the respectable salary of £20 per year. In return, he was responsible for giving them a good grounding in grammar, the classics and rhetoric – the latter particularly important at a time when eloquence mattered, both socially and in business. He would also administer a beating if they were lazy. Classes were usually conducted entirely in Latin, and a lot of the learning involved endless repetition – memorising passages until you could repeat them flawlessly, translating them into English, then returning them into Latin.

One work that the class probably studied was *On Abundance (De Copia)*. Subtitled 'the foundations of an abundant style', it was a modern bestseller by the Dutch theologian Erasmus. It looked at the many applications for even the oddest words. When you find a word, Erasmus instructs:

'...however vulgar, unusual, poetic, archaic, novel, obsolete, harsh, barbarous, or foreign it may be, lay it up in its proper niche with its fellows, so that you may summon it if ever a use for it arises.'

A larder of words – could anything be designed to appeal more strongly to the singular gifts of a young William Shakespeare?

Opposite and left: Stratford Grammar School – the main schoolroom on the upper floor of the town's Guildhall, and the inner court, adjacent to the Guild's Chapel of the Holy Cross.

Above: Desiderio Erasmus, a fresh, modern influence when Shakespeare was in school. He believed that education shouldn't depend on learning by rote, and that pupils would benefit from the exchange of ideas to broaden their thinking.

An Eye for Nature

Outside The Schoolroom
Among his contemporaries, Shakespeare has probably the greatest ability to bring the natural world onto the stage. A childhood surrounded by the sort of countryside that has almost vanished today meant he could closely observe the rural landscape, weather, plants, birds and beasts – enough material for a lifetime's writing.

Warwickshire in the mid-1500s was deeply rural – the whole county was known for being thickly wooded; in particular, the great forest of Arden was close by Stratford. Even though its trees were already being depleted by the demand for timber, this forest was still dense and wild – and it would eventually appear under its own name as the magical setting for amorous confusion in *As You Like It*.

Right: The dreamlike Forest of Arden in *As You Like It* in an early 20th-century version by the illustrator John Collier, showing Touchstone the fool courting simple Audrey, deep in the wood.

Opposite top: The frontispiece from a study of Shakespeare's knowledge of ornithology, depicting him as a falconer.

Opposite bottom: The 17th century saw a boom in zoological studies. These engravings, of a swan and a turtle dove, are taken from *Fogelboken* (The Book of Birds) from the great Swedish naturalist Olof Rudbeck.

'And this our life, exempt from public haunt,
Finds tongues in trees, books in the running brooks,
Sermons in stones, and good in everything.'

—*As You Like It*, Act 2, Scene 1

Shakespeare's knowledge was in-depth, too: more than 180 different species of animal and bird get mentions in his works; his birds are matched with accurate calls, and his plants grow where they would in nature. Nor does he make the townsman's error of seeing only an idyllic countryside. He can summon an enchanted wood for, say, *A Midsummer Night's Dream*, but he is just as much at home with the sinister, blasted heath of *Macbeth*.

A Countryman in Town

Once in London, we know that Shakespeare would be mocked as a provincial by some of his contemporaries who, with their university educations and more aristocratic connections, considered themselves a cut above him socially. However, his status as a country boy would actually serve him well in his profession. A good secondary education allied with his knowledge of the ordinary yeoman life and a keen eye for the natural world around him were a strong mix of ingredients which he would exploit to the full.

Family Matters

SIGNS OF TROUBLE
In 1577, when William would have been 13 and close to finishing grammar school, records show the first hints that John Shakespeare's fortunes had turned and he seems to have begun a slow withdrawal from civic life.

After 20 years of steady success, from the late 1570s John was a constant absentee from council meetings, and his profile as a prominent citizen of Stratford faded. It seems most likely that his difficulties arose from his unofficial side businesses – wool dealing and money lending.

Small-town Spies

Exactly what went wrong? Elizabethan England had a large and informal group of 'common informers' – semi-official spies employed by the Crown who could earn money by reporting illegal activities, especially at small-town business level. It's probable that John Shakespeare fell foul of them; in particular, his wool dealing seems to have become a large, profitable business that may have made him an easy mark for informers.

We don't have a full record of his businesses and the cases against him, but proceedings brought in the 1570s seem to have dragged on for well over a decade, draining the family of its wealth and leaving their assets constantly at risk from seizure by the Crown.

For William, the timing of John's troubles would have been difficult, coming just when he and his contemporaries would have been making decisions about their future. He may have spent his mid-teens helping in the family business; John seems to have coped with his losses by selling off what he could, as he could, so though no longer as prosperous as they had been, the Shakespeares held onto their home. In the years when a clever teenage boy might have been considering an apprenticeship or even university – neither of them free options – money had become an issue.

Money troubles or not, at the end of 1582 William Shakespeare did something that put a future as either an apprentice or a student out of reach. He got married.

Opposite: A house in busy Henley Street was the family home through Shakespeare's childhood.

Above: A desk alleged to be Shakespeare's in the Stratford classroom. Schoolboys had to bring in their own supplies of firewood and candles to ensure warmth and light while they worked.

Below: Along with his business woes, John Shakespeare was also fined for non-attendance at church – 12 silver pennies per absence. He later claimed he was avoiding people to whom he owed money.

'We have some salt of our youth in us.'

—*The Merry Wives of Windsor*, Act 2, Scene 3

Marriage and Fatherhood

A Shotgun Wedding
William Shakespeare probably married Anne Hathaway because she was expecting a child. This wasn't unusual in Tudor England – one in three brides was pregnant at the altar – and it only caused a scandal if the couple didn't marry before the birth.

Like his father, Shakespeare married a successful farmer's daughter. Anne was the oldest child of Richard Hathaway, who died the year before the marriage. A sheep farmer at Shottery, a couple of miles from Stratford, Richard left enough money for bequests for all eight of his children – in Anne's case, for a modest dowry to be paid on her marriage. At 26, the bride had reached the age at which Elizabethan couples usually married, while at 18, Shakespeare would have been considered on the young side. Married men could neither be apprenticed to a trade nor attend university, so if he had considered either of these paths, they were no longer options.

'I come to wive it wealthily in Padua;
If wealthily, then happily in Padua.'

—*The Taming of the Shrew*, Act 1, Scene 2

After the Wedding

The banns were called only once, instead of the usual three times – and the licence was granted on 27 November 1582. The couple's older daughter Susanna was born around six months later, followed by the twins, Judith and Hamnet, in 1585.

These are the events we know for certain before William Shakespeare goes missing from the record. Like so much about his life, a tiny core of more-or-less established facts is surrounded by tantalising clouds of speculation. We don't know how the couple met, or how close the relationship was. Many Shakespeare scholars believe that there can't have been much affection in a marriage where the two parties were so seldom together (and cite no further children to support an absentee father theory). Yet William and Anne remained married, and there's no reason to think they didn't live together when, later in life, he returned to spend much of his time in Stratford.

Opposite: Couples wooing, one in a 16th-century woodcut, the other a very tidy 1920s imagining of how Shakespeare and Anne Hathaway may have set about their courtship.

Below: A family of three, as in this portrait, was a small one in Shakespeare's day, leading to the long-held assumption that he and his wife spent little time together after their early years.

The 'Lost Years'

SHAKESPEARE GOES MISSING
We know that Shakespeare was in Stratford at least until 1584 – his twins were born in early 1585, so must have been conceived the year before. But after this he disappears from the record completely, going missing for seven long years.

The so-called lost years have kept historians and scholars busy for decades. Where was Shakespeare, and what was he doing? When he reappears in 1592, he is already an actor and is gaining a reputation as a playwright. He has clearly found his vocation and built the skills he needs.

Trying Out Theories

The longest-established story is that Shakespeare was caught poaching deer at the local estate, Charlecote Park, and left Stratford to escape prosecution. This might have got him to London, but it doesn't fill in what happened when he got there. Additional theories include a period in the service of a Catholic gentleman living in Lancashire – the evidence for this one depends on a staff list including 'William Shakeshafte', who seems to have been valued for his performing ability – time spent in a lawyer's office, or a period as a schoolmaster.

'This Wm. being naturally inclined to Poetry and acting, came to London I guesse about 18, and was an Actor at one of the Play-houses and did act exceedingly well.'

—John Aubrey appears to contradict his own earlier theory about William the schoolmaster, *Brief Lives*, c.1681

The schoolmaster idea was put forward in the 17th century by John Aubrey in his *Brief Lives*, but he isn't generally considered a reliable source, and he also puts forward an alternative without seeming to notice the discrepancy between the two. Another story, with a traceable connection, is that Shakespeare worked for a while in the London printshop of Richard Field. Their parents were neighbours in Stratford, the boys were probably both pupils at the grammar school and Field later published Shakespeare's poems. Inevitably this is still speculation; whatever the truth, it does seem likely that by the time we hear of Shakespeare again he had been in London for some time.

Opposite: Woodcut of an Elizabethan player, complete with stick and sword. Acting wasn't considered a respectable profession, and players were renowned for wild living.

Below: Shakespeare holds his family rapt with a dramatised reading of *Hamlet* in this Victorian engraving – an unlikely scene, as he would have been fully occupied with writing and acting professionally.

CHAPTER TWO

LIVING IN LONDON

Getting to Work

THE UPSTART CROW
The evidence that Shakespeare was based in London from 1592, and already acting and writing in the theatre there, comes from a pamphlet printed that year, called *Greene's Groatsworth of Wit.* Featuring a dramatised story, it was credited to Robert Greene, an established playwright who had died the year before.

Such pamphlets were popular, widely read and passed around between friends. It's unclear whether the whole playlet was written by Greene (some scholars attribute it even nearer to home, to Shakespeare's fellow playwright and sometime collaborator Thomas Nashe). For the modern reader the text is full of now-obscure contemporary references, and hard to follow. One passage, though, jumps out to the Shakespeare detective.

A character is warning another to watch out for London actors and their duplicitous ways:

'Yes, trust them not', he says, 'for there is an upstart Crow, beautified with our feathers, that with his Tyger's hart wrapt in a Player's hyde, supposes he is as well able to bombast out a blanke verse as the best of you; and ... is in his owne conceit the onely Shake-scene in a country.'

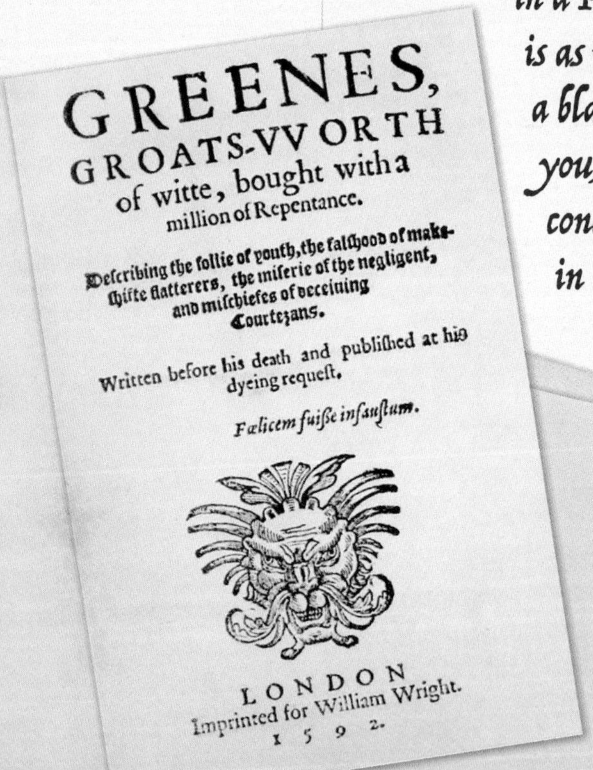
GREENES,
GROATS-VVORTH
of witte, bought with a
million of Repentance.
Describing the follie of youth, the falshood of make-
shifte flatterers, the miserie of the negligent,
and mischiefes of deceiuing
Courtezans.
Written before his death and published at his
dyeing request.
Fœlicem fuiße infaustum.
LONDON
Imprinted for William Wright.
1592.

The 'Tyger's hart' is a near-quote from Shakespeare's early play *Henry VI, Part 3*. Not only this, but the 'Shake-scene' is a clear pun on the competitor's name. The crow is accused of plagiarising London's professional writers, and the obvious conclusion is that Shakespeare is not only acting in the city in the early 1590s, but has also had the cheek, despite his lack of a university education, to set himself up as a writer of plays.

Back in Play

After such a long silence, *Greene's Groatsworth* resets the scene for us. William Shakespeare is in London, among theatre folk, and is working both as an actor and a 'maker' (playwright). It sounds as though he has been there for a time and is enjoying a degree of success – no rival would bother to write this sort of stuff about a nonentity. From this point on, Shakespeare's rise is much easier to track.

Opposite: The title page of Greene's *Groatsworth*; inside is the first – coded – mention we have of William Shakespeare as an actor and playwright.

Below: Contemporary literary feuds were often played out with the publication of witty, scurrilous pamphlets. *The Trimming of Thomas Nashe, Gentleman*, from 1571, attacks Nashe, a well-known satirist. In addition to written insults, it depicts its subject in shackles.

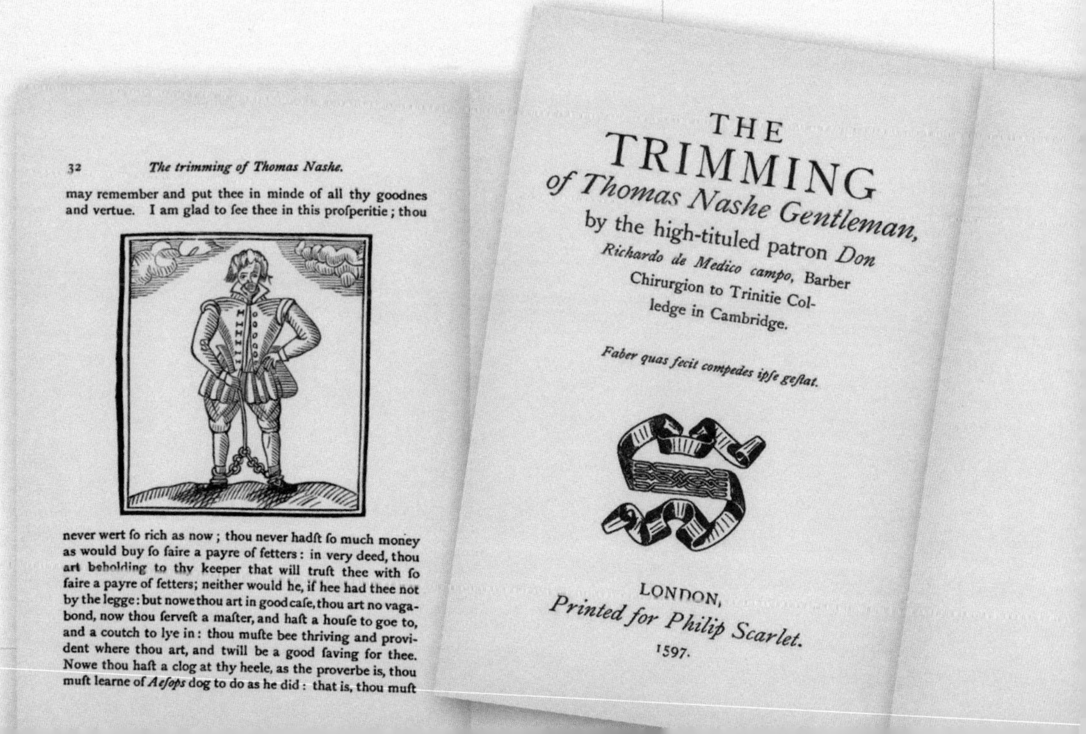

32 *The trimming of Thomas Nashe.*

may remember and put thee in minde of all thy goodnes and vertue. I am glad to ſee thee in this proſperitie; thou never wert ſo rich as now; thou never hadſt ſo much money as would buy ſo faire a payre of fetters: in very deed, thou art beholding to thy keeper that will truſt thee with ſo faire a payre of fetters; neither would he, if hee had thee not by the legge: but nowe thou art in good caſe, thou art no vagabond, now thou ſerveſt a maſter, and haſt a houſe to goe to, and a coutch to lye in: thou muſte bee thriving and provident where thou art, and twill be a good ſaving for thee. Nowe thou haſt a clog at thy heele, as the proverbe is, thou muſt learne of *Aeſops* dog to do as he did: that is, thou muſt

THE TRIMMING *of Thomas Nashe Gentleman,* by the high-tituled patron *Don Richardo de Medico campo,* Barber Chirurgion to Trinitie Colledge in Cambridge.

Faber quas fecit compedes ipſe geſtat.

LONDON,
Printed for Philip Scarlet.
1597.

A Theatrical Revolution

BRAVE NEW WORLD
The theatre in which Shakespeare had quickly found his feet was changing fast. Under Elizabeth, the who, where and what of performances were all undergoing a revolution. If you could compare working in contemporary theatre to anything today, it might have felt something like working in a start-up in a brand-new medium.

Before the 1550s, the 'theatre' most people had access to consisted of miracle or morality plays. These originated with the medieval mystery plays and were quite amateur affairs, usually performed around Christian festivals in major towns. By mid-century they were seen as uncomfortably associated with Catholicism and were being edged out by the authorities.

Royalty had a different source for their plays: boys' companies, associated with major cathedral choirs that had sung at court, had, in the reign of Henry VIII, branched out into performing classical works, and these had become a regular part of royal entertainment.

'The play's the thing...'

—*Hamlet*, Act 2, Scene 2

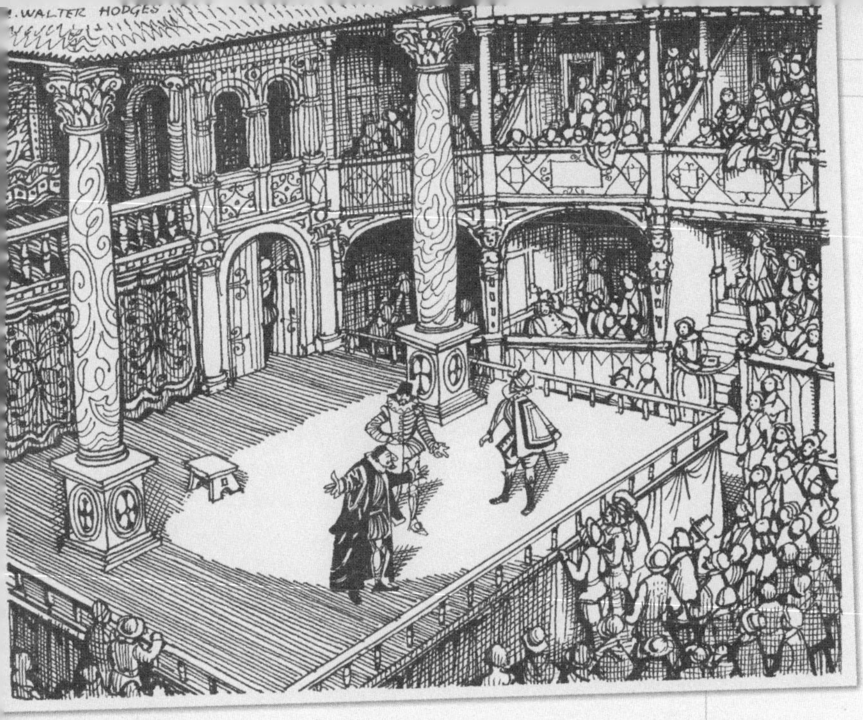

Going Professional

Other options were emerging. Between the early 1560s and '90s, professional troupes of actors were forming. These were invariably under patronage, and were named for their patron – the first, Leicester's Men, was formed in the 1550s. They performed in the capital and also went on tour, staging plays in public spaces such as guildhalls (including Stratford's), and performing privately for those who could afford to pay more. They needed formal patronage because wandering strangers were treated with suspicion and the vagrancy laws in Elizabeth's England were strongly enforced.

By the time Queen Elizabeth acquired her own troupe, the Queen's Men, in 1583, the theatre had become so popular that there was plenty of custom in London and touring was slightly less common. Specific venues were being built, and companies divided their time between 'their' theatre (many were attached to a specific group) and – if they were lucky enough to be summoned – private performances. Competition for performing at court was particularly fierce.

Opposite: Travelling players stage a show for a crowd of fascinated villagers, painted in 1542.

Above: An early custom-built theatre, with its polygonal shape, open central space for the stage and standing onlookers, and more comfortable seats under the roof for richer playgoers.

Stories and Origins

New Narratives
During the Christmas revels of 1561, Queen Elizabeth had watched a performance of the tragedy of *Gorboduc*. Set in ancient Britain, it's the tale of a king who gives his throne away to two warring sons. Most of the characters end up dead.

More actors were entering the profession and the plays in which they acted were changing, too. They fell loosely into three categories – comedies, tragedies and histories, the latter taken from the classics as well as more modern times and sometimes treating the historical aspect of 'history' very loosely indeed. Near-unreadable today, *Gorboduc* was groundbreaking because it was the first play written in blank verse, in English. Its plot had been taken from the work of the 12th-century historian Geoffrey of Monmouth.

Greatest Hits

Shakespeare's fame has far outgrown that of his contemporaries, so it's easy to forget that he was entering a crowded field. Fashions were moving fast, too – in 1588 the playwright John Lyly produced *Endymion*, a classical allegory constructed both to show off the author's erudition and to flatter that of his audience. It was performed before the Queen, to great acclaim, by the Children of Paul's (the boys' troupe attached to St Paul's Cathedral) at Greenwich Palace in 1588.

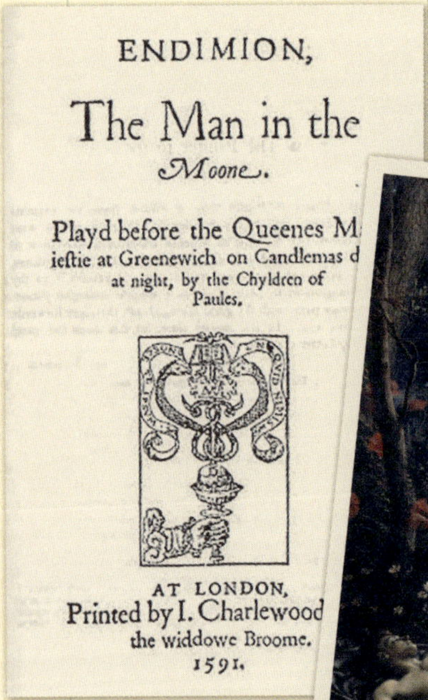
ENDIMION,
The Man in the
Moone.
Playd before the Queenes M
iestie at Greenewich on Candlemas d
at night, by the Chyldren of
Paules.
AT LONDON,
Printed by I. Charlewood
the widdowe Broome.
1591.

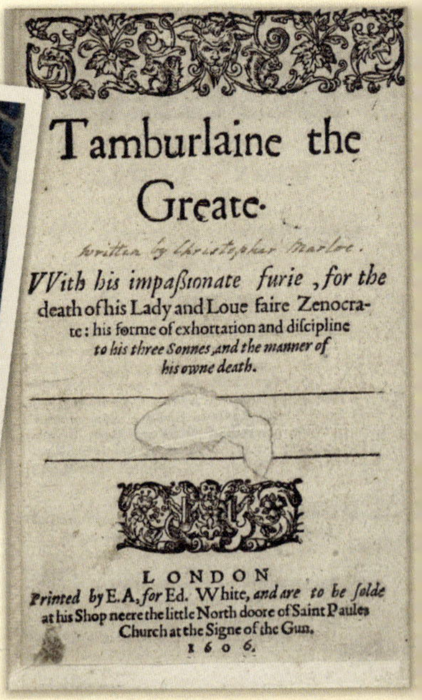
Tamburlaine the
Greate.
Written by Christopher Marlowe.
VVith his impaßionate furie, for the
death of his Lady and Loue faire Zenocra-
te: his forme of exhortation and discipline
to his three Sonnes, and the manner of
his owne death.
LONDON
Printed by E.A, for Ed. White, and are to be solde
at his Shop neere the little North doore of Saint Paules
Church at the Signe of the Gun.
1606.

Different qualities, though, were soon taking centre stage, even at court. Christopher Marlowe's *Tamburlaine the Great* made its first appearance in the late 1580s, while Thomas Kyd's *Spanish Tragedy*, the first in a whole new class of revenge tragedies, would appear in 1592. These muscular stories, offering plenty of action told in powerful but – comparatively – straightforward language show the way the wind was blowing.

When it came to finding stories, the new writers were magpies, picking up likely plots wherever they could find them, and taking any liberties needed to make them work. Plots were often repurposed, too – the *True Tragedie of Richard the third* and *King Leir* were both performed on London's stages well before Shakespeare's versions appeared.

'Vengeance is in my heart, death in my hand.'

—*Titus Andronicus*, Act 2, Scene 3

Opposite: The title pages of *Endymion* and *Tamburlaine the Great*, shown with a 20th-century illustration of the classical myth behind *Endymion*. *Tamburlaine* was the more novel of the two, carrying onlookers along with its gripping story.

Below: A contemporary sketch of the Swan Theatre, built for London theatregoers in Bankside in 1595.

Poet and Patron

Earning During Plague Years

The theatre world was thriving but couldn't escape the plague; between 1592 and 1594 London saw repeated bad outbreaks. When the authorities closed the theatres, William Shakespeare would have been forced to explore alternative options.

Unlike the confused sequence and dating of many of his plays and sonnets, the dates of his two long-form poems are nailed down – *Venus and Adonis* was published in 1593, *The Rape of Lucrece* the following year. Both were dedicated to a new patron, Henry Wriothesley, the Earl of Southampton.

Southampton was 20 in 1593, 10 years Shakespeare's junior, and an educated, fashionable man-about-court with an enthusiasm for the theatre. We don't know how the two met, but it seems reasonable to guess it was at a court performance.

'I know not how I shall offend in dedicating my unpolished lines to your Lordship, nor how the world will censure me for choosing so strong a prop to support so weak a burden.'

—From the dedication to *Venus and Adonis*, 1593

Sources and Profit

The poems have classical inspiration – Ovid and Livy – and quite erotic subject matter. They were printed by Richard Field, Shakespeare's old contact from Stratford, who sold them in the larger, upmarket folio format. *Venus and Adonis* in particular was a standout bestseller over a long period – by 1640 it would be into a sixteenth printing, almost unprecedented for the times. Even with the high cost of printing, it must have been an earner – the single recorded purchase was by a Richard Stonley, who noted he had paid 12 pennies for a copy. Southampton wouldn't necessarily have rewarded the dedications directly, but it wasn't unusual for patrons to give financial presents if an author was in need.

The two poems put Shakespeare's work on the page for the first time – and, perhaps surprisingly to us, cemented an early reputation as a fashionable poet, showcasing the skill and vibrancy of his writing before he was much known as a playwright at all.

Opposite: Shakespeare's glamorous patron, the Earl of Southampton, painted in 1603 with his cat Trixie, during a confinement in the Tower after he had unwisely supported the rebellion of the Earl of Essex.

Below: The vibrant writing of *Venus and Adonis* – and its sexy subject matter – meant that for a time Shakespeare was more widely known as a poet than a playwright.

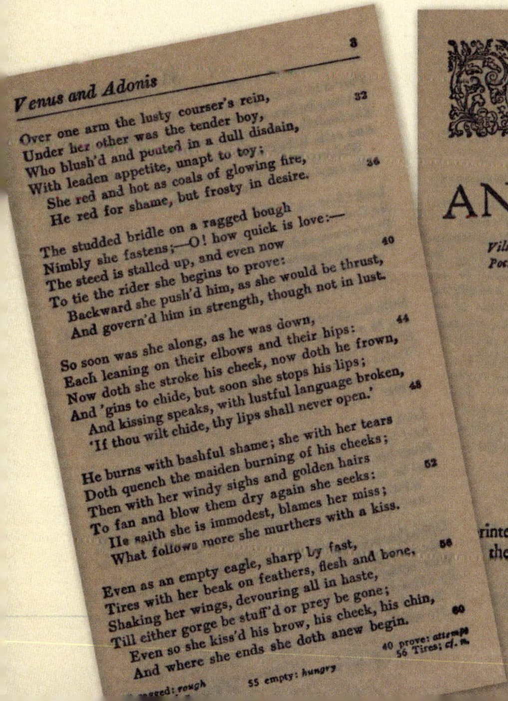
Venus and Adonis 3

Over one arm the lusty courser's rein,
Under her other was the tender boy,
Who blush'd and pouted in a dull disdain,
With leaden appetite, unapt to toy;
She red and hot as coals of glowing fire,
He red for shame, but frosty in desire.

The studded bridle on a ragged bough
Nimbly she fastens;—O! how quick is love:—
The steed is stalled up, and even now
To tie the rider she begins to prove:
Backward she push'd him, as she would be thrust,
And govern'd him in strength, though not in lust.

So soon was she along, as he was down,
Each leaning on their elbows and their hips:
Now doth she stroke his cheek, now doth he frown,
And 'gins to chide, but soon she stops his lips;
And kissing speaks, with lustful language broken,
'If thou wilt chide, thy lips shall never open.'

He burns with bashful shame; she with her tears
Doth quench the maiden burning of his cheeks;
Then with her windy sighs and golden hairs
To fan and blow them dry again she seeks:
He saith she is immodest, blames her miss;
What follows more she murthers with a kiss.

Even as an empty eagle, sharp by fast,
Tires with her beak on feathers, flesh and bone,
Shaking her wings, devouring all in haste,
Till either gorge be stuff'd or prey be gone;
Even so she kiss'd his brow, his cheek, his chin,
And where she ends she doth anew begin.

ragged: rough 55 empty: hungry 40 prove: attempt 56 Tires; cf. n.

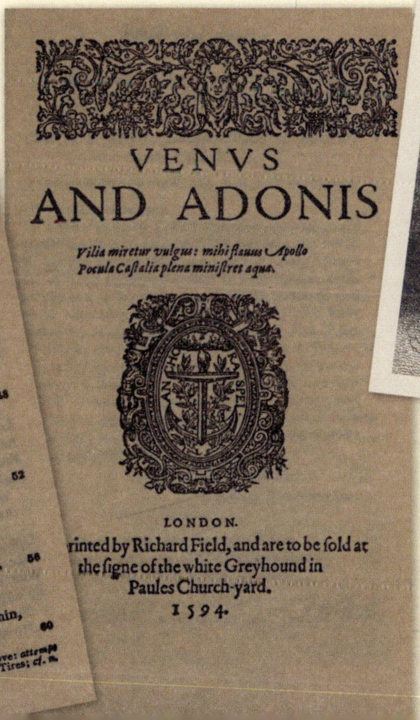
VENVS
AND ADONIS

Vilia miretur vulgus: mihi flauus Apollo
Pocula Castalia plena ministret aqua.

LONDON.
rinted by Richard Field, and are to be sold at
the signe of the white Greyhound in
Paules Church-yard.
1594.

Starting Out

The Early Works
It's generally agreed that the three parts of *Henry VI*, plus *The Comedy of Errors* and *Titus Andronicus*, were among Shakespeare's first plays. But their timeline is a jigsaw, to be pieced together cautiously.

Scholars have sought out notes on possible first performances, comments from other playwrights and so on. Taking the three-part history first: it's likely that *Henry VI* wasn't written in chronological order: *Parts 2* and *3* having scored an unexpected success, *Part 1* was written to cash in on their popularity – much as today's creators of a hit TV series may put together a prequel later. Its contemporary popularity has fallen off sharply since – certainly the later *Henry V* is much easier for us to admire – but history plays were seen as topical and could be used as vehicles for patriotism, complete with coded references to current affairs.

Titus Andronicus – an unrelievedly grim, Roman-set tale featuring rape, murder and a cannibal pie, all borrowed from a mixture of bastardised classical and medieval sources – seems to have been performed by Sussex's Men, under the management of Philip Henslowe, at the Rose Theatre in 1594. Later that year, it would become the first of Shakespeare's plays to be printed.

'For now I stand as one upon a rock, Environed with a wilderness of sea'

—*Titus Andronicus*, Act 3, Scene I

Classical Principles

The Comedy of Errors features two pairs of twins muddling their way through the plot. The language is already rich; the story, though, feels oddly flat. Classicists will recognise that Shakespeare is sticking to the Aristotelian principles of drama, learned at grammar school – he's relying on compressing the timeframe of the play and limiting it to one location to give it the greatest impact. Later he will be confident enough to move away from the guidelines, with glorious results.

Few would argue that these plays are Shakespeare's best, but they let us see him at work: how to show history on stage (the *Henrys*), how to work your audience for shock value (*Titus*) and how to structure a classic comedy (*Comedy of Errors*). We're standing by the stage watching the great playwright's learning curve.

Left: The impresario Philip Henslowe was first to build a theatre, the Rose, in Bankside, in 1587. Some of Shakespeare's early works, including *Titus Andronicus* and *Henry VI* were staged here.

Above right: *The Comedy of Errors* is the first – though far from the last – of Shakespeare's plays propelled by comic misunderstandings around a pair, or pairs, of identical twins.

Right: The bloody classical story behind *Titus Andronicus* would already have been familiar to many Shakespearean audiences.

Actor and Playwright

A Company Man?
Over the early 1590s Shakespeare published two popular, long-form poems and wrote a number of plays. He somehow weathered the long closures of the London theatres between 1592 and early 1594. But where did he live, what was he doing day-to-day and was he attached to a particular troupe?

There were quite a few companies in the 1590s and the regularity with which personnel moved around, plus incomplete records, makes it very hard to track who belonged to which troupe and when. However, scholars have plausibly placed Shakespeare with two companies during this period.

Acting Connections

The first is Lord Strange's Men, who performed the brand-new 'harey the vi', believed to be *Henry VI, Part I,* at their base, the Rose Theatre, early in 1592, just before it was closed because of plague. The second is Pembroke's Men, a company under the patronage of Henry Herbert, the Earl of Pembroke. Their performance record shows that they were the first – in some cases the only – troupe to stage Shakespeare's other early works. Both *Titus Andronicus* and *Parts 2* and *3* of *Henry VI* appear on their performance records. Being a company member offered some stability, unlike the lot of a jobbing playwright who had to tout individual plays to different

companies. And as a company member, Shakespeare would have been both writing and acting, and likely would also have joined Pembroke's Men on their so-called Plague Tour, performing in the provinces in 1592 and '93.

Many Londoners were keen to leave town during the worst plague outbreaks, but although the Plague Tour visited some prestigious locations – including the stunning Hardwick Hall, newly built home of Bess, Countess of Shrewsbury – it does not seem to have been a commercial success. And shortly after their return to London, Shakespeare made a positive move – to the company that would serve him well for the next two decades, the Lord Chamberlain's Men.

Opposite: London buries its dead. In a bad plague year, the graveyards overflowed and burials were moved outside the city boundaries.

Below: Hardwick Hall, which hosted some performances on the Plague Tour, including the popular *Henry VI*. The illustration is from *Henry VI, Part 2*, showing Richard of Gloucester, the character who would become one of Shakespeare's greatest villains in *Richard III*.

'Speak the speech, I pray you, as I pronounced it to you, trippingly on the tongue.'

—*Hamlet*, Act 2, Scene 3

Burbage and Sons

A Theatrical Pioneer
So strongly would the two become linked that it becomes impossible to tell the story of Shakespeare's life in London theatre without looking at the background of the Burbage family – James and his two sons.

James was apprenticed as a carpenter, but in the early 1570s he had joined the Earl of Leicester's Men as an actor. He toured with them before setting up on his own, leasing a plot (from Giles Allen, a Puritan who, like many of his faith, disapproved of its subsequent use) in Shoreditch in 1576 and using his carpentry contacts to raise a private, purpose-built theatre on it. Public performances were prohibited within the City, but Shoreditch was just outside it, so Burbage wasn't constrained by the rules.

James Burbage doesn't seem to have been an easy man. He was quick to anger and, in his early days in the theatre, in constant conflict with John Brayne, who was not only his business partner but also his brother-in-law. But he was a genuine entrepreneur, one of the first great theatre owners. He had plenty of drive, and he got things done.

'...can this cockpit hold
The vasty fields of France? Or may we cram
Within this wooden O the very casques
That did affright the air at Agincourt?'

—*Henry V*, Prologue

A New Style of Theatre

Unimaginatively named The Theatre, the building was a three-storey polygon with a thatched roof to protect richer patrons, an open stage in the centre and two exterior staircases to reach the upper floors. Performances took place in the afternoon; daylight was needed to light the stage. Several different troupes played there – Leicester's Men, with their connection to James Burbage were probably the first, followed in the 1580s by the Admiral's Men. In 1594, Richard Burbage, James's younger son and by now a celebrated actor, would become part of the newly formed Lord Chamberlain's Men, which Shakespeare joined the same year. And before the company moved bases, The Theatre saw the debut performances of several of Shakespeare's plays.

Opposite top: Reconstruction and plan of The Theatre as it could have appeared in the late 1570s. The Shoreditch setting may not have been as bucolic as this, but it was safely outside the city boundaries.

Opposite bottom: A 20th-century illustration of a Tudor play staging in an innyard. Innyards in reality were usually too busy for this to be possible, and if there was no theatre, stagings were more likely in rented public buildings or grand, private homes.

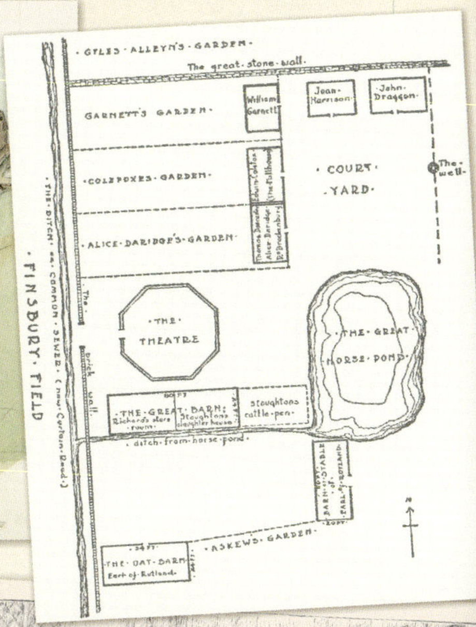
· GYLES · ALLEYN'S · GARDEN ·
The great · stone · wall.
GARNETT'S GARDEN ·
William Garnett
Jean · Harrison ·
· John · Draggon ·
· COLEFOXES · GARDEN ·
Edwin Colston
· COURT ·
· YARD ·
The · well ·
· ALICE · DARIDGE'S · GARDEN ·
Thomas Daridge
Alice Daridge
· THE · DITCH · or · COMMON · SEWER · (now · Curtain · Road ·)
· FINSBURY · FIELD
The ·
· THE ·
THEATRE
brick wall.
· THE · GREAT · HORSE · POND ·
· THE · GREAT · BARN ·
Richard's store · room ·
Stoughtons slaughter house
Stoughtons cattle · pen ·
· ditch · from · horse · pond ·
BARN · or · STABLE · of · EARL · of · RUTLAND ·
· ASKEWS · GARDEN ·
· THE · OAT · BARN ·
Earl · of · Rutland ·

The Lord Chamberlain's Men

THE NOBLE COMPANY
From its foundation in 1594, the Lord Chamberlain's Men would become the preeminent and longest-lived theatrical company in England, lasting through a renaming as the King's Men – on the accession of James I in 1603 – all the way until the outbreak of civil war in 1642.

The company had a complicated birth, sparked by the natural moving and shaking that took place when theatres reopened for business after being closed for most of the previous two years. Its patron was Henry Carey, Lord Chamberlain to the Queen. Part of his role was to take charge of royal entertainments, so his troupe were automatically in a good position for invitations to perform for the court.

A New Line-up

Two of its most important members, Richard Burbage and Will Kempe, a well-known comic actor, had been with Lord Strange's Men, who broke up after their patron's death, shortly before the new company's foundation. Twenty-seven-year-old Burbage would be the company's leading man – an excellent actor, tall, imposing and able to tackle any heroic role, especially a tragic

one, while Kempe, a few years older, small and tubby, was already a renowned clown, a leading comic actor loved by audiences for his rude jokes and capers in the jig at the end of a play. And in William Shakespeare they had a playwright who had already proved his versatility and who was just embarking on his mature work.

Shakespeare was one of eight 'sharers' in the Lord Chamberlain's Men – as a sharer in the company, you pooled your assets, shared the costs and took an income out of what was left. In a successful company, you could become a rich man.

Unsurprisingly the new company seems to have performed at The Theatre, owned by Richard's father, as well as The Curtain, nearby, and, briefly in 1594, at a new theatre at Newington Butts.

Opposite left: Richard Burbage became a universally popular leading man; when he died in 1619, the whole of London seems to have gone into mourning.

Opposite right: The new theatres were growing more sophisticated to match the new companies. Here, the stage is backed by a curtained 'tiring house', a concealed space where the players could change and spare props were stored.

Below: A contemporary woodcut of Will Kempe, dressed in his easily recognisable Fool's motley and bells, dancing one of his famous jigs.

'The better part of valour is discretion, in the which better part I have saved my life.'

—*Henry IV, Part 1*, Act 5, Scene 4

Company Roles

WHO DID WHAT
The Lord Chamberlain's Men would be a particularly successful company; that it lasted so long means that it was also an efficient one. Although company roles wouldn't match those in the theatre today, everyone knew what was expected of them. They must have regularly multitasked, too.

Sharers were actors – Shakespeare acted as well as writing – who also took a share in management. Under them were hired men – actors who were paid but didn't share in the profits. They needed to be flexible: able to dance, play an instrument, and, if there weren't enough dedicated stagehands, to help to shift things about and produce the sound effects (although Elizabethan theatre didn't have much scenery, it did create excellent warfare and storm noises, sometimes, dangerously, using gunpowder). The youngest company members were the apprentices, teenage boys whose unbroken voices were needed in female parts.

Mastering a Part

Shakespeare's oddest stage direction – 'Exit, pursued by a bear' from *The Winter's Tale* – has gained a fame of its own, but detailed directions were actually very rare, and actors had a large amount of discretion. The role of director didn't really exist, and players didn't get a complete script; instead, they got their own lines, with short cues to tell them when to come in. With the number of plays being performed (often a different play every day of the week), time for rehearsals was limited. A player who had his part

Archidamus

Camillo

'Since I was man,
Such sheets of fire,
such bursts of horrid thunder,
Such groans of roaring wind
and rain I never
Remember to have heard.'

—*King Lear*, Act 3, Scene 2

'under his belt' had learned his lines and tucked away the papers on which they were written.

Costumes often originated from aristocratic households – when clothes went out of fashion, lords and ladies passed them on to servants, who sold them on to the players. There wouldn't have been much attempt at historical accuracy, but the costumes' grand origins gave the option for a king, say, to be appropriately richly dressed.

Opposite left: A Victorian engraving of *The Winter's Tale*'s Antigonus, pursued by a literal bear – unlikely to have been the case even on the Shakespearean stage.

Above left: Lear and his Fool by the great illustrator Arthur Rackham. Storms and tempests offered great opportunities for contemporary sound effects.

Below: Paper costumes created in the 19th century for a toy theatre version of *The Winter's Tale*. Three centuries earlier real stage costumes would have been much simpler.

The Rivals

THE ADMIRAL'S MEN
It might not have seemed possible that another company could compete with the Lord Chamberlain's Men. Around the same time that they came together, though, the Admiral's Men were also on the rise.

In many ways, the strengths of the Admiral's Men mirrored those of the Lord Chamberlain's Men. They both had a prominent patron and a theatrical impresario; they both also had a standout leading man and a connection to a particularly talented playwright. All enough to make comparisons interesting, and for a few years in the 1590s, the two were by far the most prestigious companies performing in London.

Who's Who

The Admiral leading the company was Charles Howard, Earl of Nottingham, who had been appointed England's Lord High Admiral in 1585. The impresario was Philip Henslowe, proprietor of the Rose Theatre, built in 1587 and sited close to The Theatre. The leading man was Edward Alleyn, like Richard Burbage a performer powerful enough to pull in an audience – and, not entirely coincidentally, Henslowe's son-in-law. And the playwright often favoured by the company was the celebrated, scandalous Christopher Marlowe.

For a brief summer in 1594 the companies actually shared the theatre at Newington Butts and may even have swapped works (it's here that *The Taming of the Shrew* was probably first performed – by the Admiral's Men) but they soon withdrew to their respective theatres, each keeping an eye on their competitors' output. When the Admiral's Men regularly repeated Marlowe's *Doctor Faustus*, the tale of a soul sold, with its fabulous ending of devils dragging its anti-hero off to hell, the Lord Chamberlain's Men played the similarly fantastical *A Midsummer Night's Dream*, which Shakespeare probably created for an aristocratic wedding, but which proved a runaway hit in regular performance. Was there a conscious rivalry? It's hard to imagine anything else. And it probably had a good effect on the creativity of both companies.

Opposite left: The source story of Dr Faustus and his disastrous pact appeared in a 1590s German work; Christopher Marlowe, opposite right, made it into a huge hit on stage.

Below: Edward Alleyn, the only other leading man in London who was considered to rival Richard Burbage. He starred in both *Faustus* and *Tamburlaine*.

'In cases of defence, 'tis best to weigh The enemy more mighty than he seems'

—*Henry V*, Act 2, Scene 3

The Taming of the Shrew

A Successful Comedy
On 11 June 1594, Philip Henslowe recorded that '*the tamynge of A shrowe*', for which he had paid 9 shillings, had been performed at the Newington Butts Theatre. This was probably one of the earliest performances of Shakespeare's *Shrew*, and the play has been popular pretty much ever since.

As usual, tracking back to Shakespeare's original isn't easy. The *Shrew* familiar to us only appears in the First Folio, the posthumous collection of his plays, but something that might be a pirated version, or just an early one – *A Pleasant Conceited* (meaning cunning, well-put-together) *Historie, called The taming of a Shrew* was printed and sold in 1594. It has no named author. Scholars now think this was an early version of Shakespeare's play, and it's probably the one that was being performed.

Marriage Matters

By later Shakespearean standards, *Shrew* is still slightly rough structurally. It sets up a play-within-a-play with Christopher Sly – a tinker duped into believing he's a lord – as audience of one

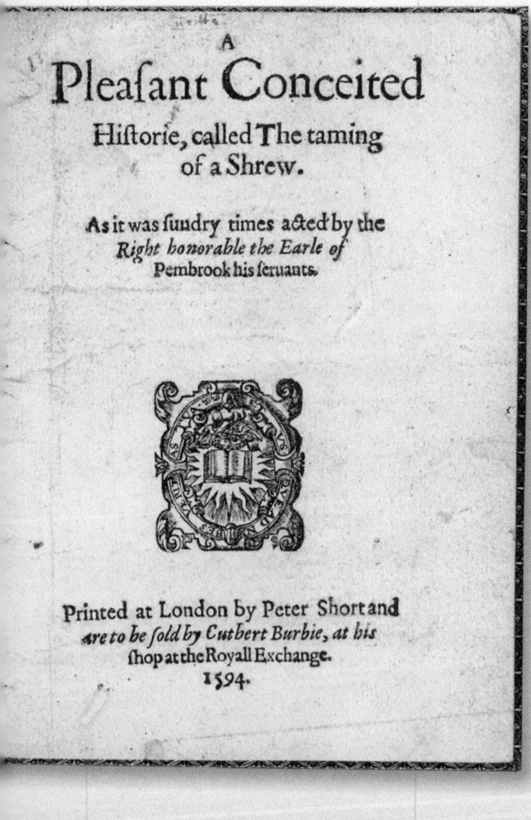
A
Pleaſant Conceited
Hiſtorie, called The taming
of a Shrew.

As it was ſundry times acted by the
Right honorable the Earle of
Pembrook his ſeruants.

Printed at London by Peter Short and
are to be ſold by Cutbert Burbie, at his
ſhop at the Royall Exchange.
1594.

'...when she is froward,
peevish, sullen, sour,
And not obedient
to his honest will,
What is she but a
foul contending rebel
And graceless traitor
to her loving lord?'

—*The Taming of the Shrew*, Act 5, Scene 2

to the main action, but then wanders off as we become absorbed in the good wife/bad wife central story and the numerous deceptions and mistaken identities. 'Taming' a wife would have seemed acceptable, indeed necessary, to a Tudor audience, 'shrew' implies a nag; no Elizabethan spouse would want her to graduate to a scold, a much harsher category.

This comedy's action is propelled much more effectively than that of, say, *The Comedy of Errors*, and the final irony of good girl Bianca proving to be a shrew in her own right is an enjoyable turning of the tables. Shakespeare has skilfully got us rooting for the Petruchio/Katherine union: even as she declares humility, Katherine still presents as outspoken and confident, qualities that keep the play watchable today.

Opposite: The 1594 title page of the first *Shrew*, which is believed to be an early version of Shakespeare's play.

Below: Petruchio's confected rage frightens his servants and even intimidates Katherine – a key scene, painted in 1861 by Sir John Gilbert.

Going to the Theatre

An Everyday Pleasure
When neither plague nor anti-theatre Puritans had caused their temporary closure, the theatres had no trouble drawing in the crowds. Many Londoners went weekly on afternoon visits; performances started from around 2pm.

What a theatre visit was like depended somewhat on what you could afford. The hoi polloi (those that had a penny, the basic price of admission), known as groundlings, would be jostled together, probably without much of a view of the stage. Tuppence got you a seat and a better view. Another penny meant a good seat in the gallery with a cushion on it. Refreshments were noisily hawked throughout the performance and if the play proved unpopular, people would be free with their comments. Sometimes they threw things. Elizabethan actors had to be resilient.

Some of the managers' records reveal that the theatres could get unbelievably – and dangerously – crowded during performances: a building that might be reckoned to hold 700 people comfortably regularly totted up entrance fees from an audience of closer to 2,000. Add to this that theatres were sited in insalubrious areas, often in among the city's bearpits and brothels, and it is small wonder that they had a bad name, with constant complaints of pickpockets, groping and lawless disorder.

'I have often seen, after the finishing of some worthy tragedy... that the scene after the Epilogue hath been more blacke ~ a nasty bawdy jigge ~ than the most horrid scene in the play was.'

—Thomas Dekker, tragedian, failing to appreciate light relief at the end of the play, 1613

Happy Endings

The play was the main event, but when it finished, there was a small extra show, a 'jig', which might be a short, complete piece or a few separate skits. Both options would have plenty of lewd jokes, and would incorporate music and dancing. If the performing company had a standout comic actor, this was a chance for him to do his turn and send the audience home happy – even if they'd just watched a harrowing tragedy.

Opposite: The Globe was across the way from Southwark's bearpit – watching dogs fighting bears was as popular an entertainment as a visit to the theatre.

Below left: Even the new purpose-built theatres didn't offer great views for the humble standing groundlings.

Below: Originally a member of the Queen's Players and a favourite with Elizabeth, Richard Tarlton was an early comic actor, father of the jig. He died in 1588; Will Kempe was his successor as London's popular 'jestmonger'.

Private Performances

Going Upmarket
Invitations to perform for the court were the most prestigious bookings that an acting company could get. The monarch never went to the theatre: Elizabeth usually watched plays at the palaces of Whitehall or Greenwich, or, occasionally, at the houses of one or other of her favoured courtiers.

A troupe performing privately did so under different circumstances from their everyday routine. Court performances often took place at night – here, there was no difficulty with lighting: chandeliers loaded with candles surrounded the stage. Banked seats ensured that everyone had a good view, with the Queen presiding from a chair at the front. Before the performance, a rehearsal was held for the Master of Revels (who underpinned the Lord Chamberlain's role and managed a lot of practical aspects of court entertainment) so that he could check its suitability and suggest any cuts he felt were necessary.

Court stagings might feature dancing and music, but they dispensed with the vulgar jig at the end of the play – often it would be hastily replaced by a specially written Epilogue, which might compliment the Queen and the aristocratic audience.

'A company of base and common Fellows, to make up our Disorders with a Play of Errors and Confusions.'

—A poor write-up of the December 1594 performance – punning on the title of the play – from the records book of entertainments held at Gray's Inn

A Night of Errors

Things did sometimes go wrong. Popular theatre companies had plenty of private bookings other than court ones – they often performed, for example, before the resident lawyers and law students at Gray's Inn, where their skilled oratory would have been fully appreciated. On 28 December 1594, the Lord Chamberlain's Men were booked to perform *The Comedy of Errors* at Gray's Inn but were subsequently summoned to Greenwich Palace to play before the Queen. Instead of sensibly cancelling Gray's Inn, they tried to squeeze in both, playing at court first and only showing up for the lawyers after midnight, by which time the audience was drunk and the stage had been dismantled. They did the play anyway, to less-than-favourable reviews.

Opposite: A 19th-century imagining of the Lord Chamberlain's Men performing before the Queen. Court stagings were much more intimate affairs than theatre performances.

Top: Gray's Inn, where players were guaranteed a cultured audience in the lawyers, if sometimes a rowdy one.

Above: A 19th-century German engraving of costume designs for *Twelfth Night*. Sebastian is on the left; Malvolio, identifiable by his yellow stockings, is far right.

Playing by the Rules

LICENCES AND CENSORSHIP
You might imagine that producing plays was simpler in the age before copyright. You'd be wrong – playwrights in Elizabethan England operated under quite strict censorship.

A new play must be submitted to the Master of Revels, who worked under the Lord Chamberlain, to be granted a licence (when it was to be performed at court, there was an approval rehearsal, too). An influential patron was helpful – of course, if that patron was the Lord Chamberlain himself, it would ease the way. Anything that hinted at a departure from Church of England orthodoxy was censored, and plays featuring lax morality, dodgy political views or serious oaths also risked being banned, or at least heavily edited.

Running into Trouble

Shakespeare didn't always manage to avoid problems. The whole abdication scene in *Richard II* was cut because the abdication of a monarch went against the perceived natural order of things. Generally, he was clever and subtle; whenever you see him sailing close to the wind – with the regicide in *Macbeth* for example – he makes sure he has a character on hand to point out the correct view of the case.

'[I recall] the strange turning of The Isle of Dogs from a comedy to a tragedy two summers past, with the troublesome stir which happened about it...'

—Thomas Nashe remembers the episode nonchalantly, perhaps because, unlike his colleagues, he managed to stay out of prison, 1599

We know of only one play that seems to have escaped the censor completely. Performed by Pembroke's Men in 1597, it caused real trouble. Called *The Isle of Dogs*, it was authored, not by sensible Shakespeare, but by Thomas Nashe and Ben Jonson. Maddeningly we don't have any details about what was wrong with it and no copy survives – maybe it openly disrespected Elizabeth herself – but it was abruptly cancelled, amid a huge ruckus, and Jonson and two of his fellow actors were sent to Marshalsea Prison, although eventually the scandal died down and they were released.

Opposite: Henry Carey, Elizabeth I's valued courtier and patron of the Lord Chamberlain's Men.

Above: Shakespeare and Ben Jonson were friends as well as colleagues. Here, they're seen playing chess in a 1913 painting by De Heyman.

Below: Playwrights or actors who took too many risks might find themselves confined in the Marshalsea Prison, seen here; a formal pardon was needed to get them out.

Publishing Plays

MISSING PLAYS

Today it's estimated that of around 3,000 plays written and performed between the 1580s and the closure of the theatres in 1642, all but about 550 are lost. The ones that survive only did so because they had been printed.

Although playwrights were kept busy producing a constant supply of works to feed a ravenous audience, a new play for a company was jealously guarded – there was a single master copy, passed from the playwright to the 'bookkeeper', a company member who kept it safe and held it during rehearsals and performances, ready to prompt if necessary. This would be the 'correct' copy, but each actor knew only their own part, and any glitches would have been covered by improvisation. Plays were seen as ephemeral entertainment rather than gospel – different versions of different stories abounded, and early versions of many plays that we'd think of as set in stone were often full of mistakes, variations and cuts.

'Life's but a walking shadow, a poor player,
That struts and frets his hour upon the stage,
And then is heard no more.'

—*Macbeth*, Act 5, Scene 5

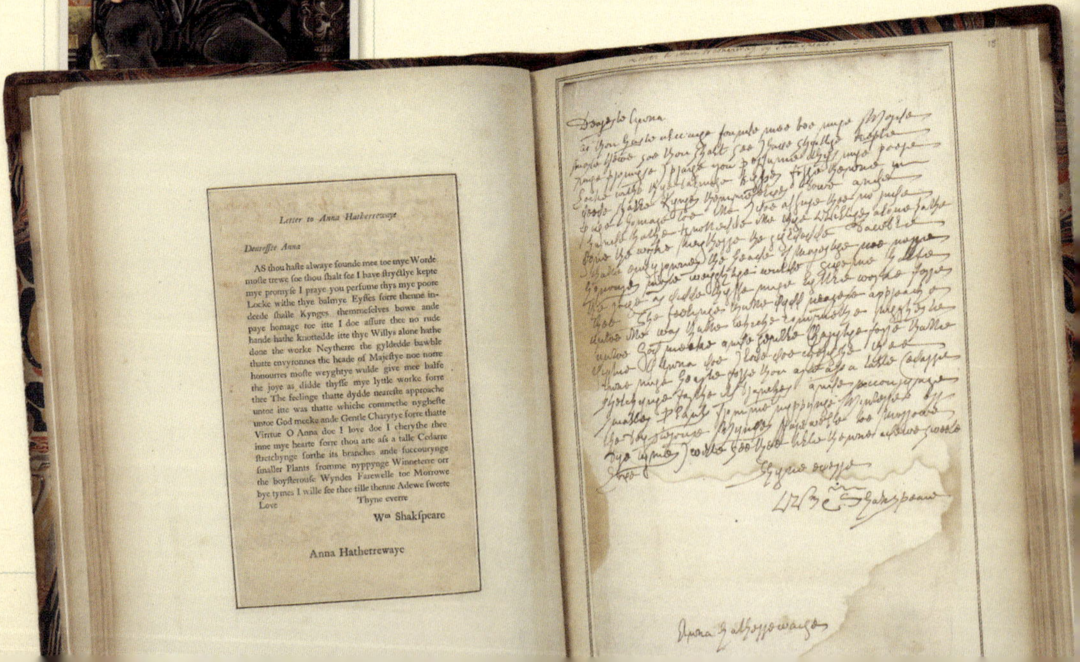

How Plays Got Into Print

Piracy was also rife: an unscrupulous actor could memorise most of a play and take it to a rival company or even sell it to a printer (the wildly bodged versions that emerged from this sort of deal were known as 'bad quartos'). Alternatively, a company might sell a printer a play that had done particularly well for them when they felt they had had the best out of it – in which case, the result was a 'good quarto' – that is, a more or less accurate version of what had been seen on stage. The printed plays that survive often don't name the author – but frequently mention the acting company who performed them. From 1586, a printer had to have a licence from the Stationers Company, the official publishing body, to print a work, too, which made for an additional expense.

Finally, those playwrights who became famous might have their collected works printed in the larger, costlier folio size – as was the case with Ben Jonson and, posthumously, Shakespeare. But this was the crowning achievement of a successful career and was far from the norm.

Opposite top: Victorian portrait of Shakespeare.

Opposite bottom: William Henry Ireland is the most famous forger of Shakespeare. He began with signatures, moved on to letters and eventually created an entire 'lost' play, *Vortigern*. The latter was quite unlike anything by Shakespeare and was laughed off stage at its first performance in 1796, prompting Ireland to make a full confession.

Below: The Dering Manuscript, a script for *Henry IV, Parts 1* and *2*, combined and much shortened. It seems to have been created in the 1620s for a private performance at the home of Sir Edward Dering – the earliest example of country house theatricals.

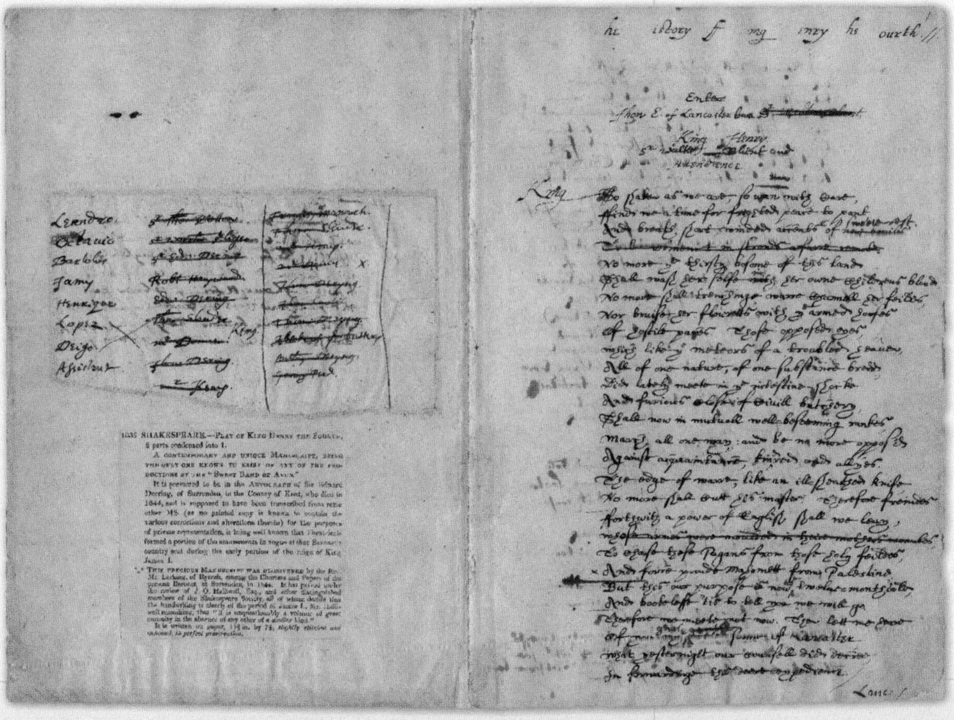

Richard II

A Popular History
***Richard II* was first performed in 1595 and went into print in an abbreviated form two years later. By 1608, still apparently popular in performance, it had been printed again, this time full-length and with the playwright's credit on the cover.**

It seems to have been a hit from its first outing. Richard II's story would have been familiar to a Tudor audience, and the plot would have held some of the contemporary resonance that made history plays popular. They knew that Richard had been dethroned, and that his forced abdication left the way free for Henry Bolingbroke who would become King Henry IV, an effective ruler who won great victories in France. But the idea that one ruler might seize power from another, regardless of the latter's anointed right to rule, might have rung alarm bells at court.

Dangerous Precedents

Famously, the abdication scene was cut from early performances of the play. By the time it was written, Elizabeth I was into her 60s, long past the age of childbearing. The charm of a Virgin Queen had worn thin, and she was obstinately refusing to name her successor, which made her more vulnerable to enemies.

'I am Richard II, know ye not that?', she is supposed to have said in 1601 to her archivist, William Lambarde, in the wake of the rebellion and subsequent execution of her one-time favourite, the Earl of Essex.

This is the history play in which we start to feel Shakespeare's mature skill. He confidently wrestles his way around the knotty plot, aware of all the nuances between strong and weak personalities. Along the way, he creates some of his most powerful word pictures of kingship and kingdom, perhaps most memorably in the long speech given by John of Gaunt, Richard's uncle, raising the image of England as 'this precious stone set in the silver sea'.

Opposite: Richard II, shown visiting a dying John of Gaunt, against the title page of the second edition, published – with an author's credit – in 1608.

Below: An unflattering portrait of Elizabeth I, painted by Marcus Gheeraerts the Younger in 1595, when she was 62 years old. Her elaborate dress can't disguise her tired appearance.

***'With mine own tears
I wash away my balm,
With mine own hands
I give away my crown.'***

—*Richard II*, Act 4, Scene 1

CHAPTER THREE

A LIFE IN THEATRE

Back in Stratford

Home News
From 1594 we can track the main events of Shakespeare's career by following the Lord Chamberlain's Men. What was going on in Stratford isn't so clear, although one sad event would have affected the whole family. Aged 11, Hamnet Shakespeare died.

According to the Holy Trinity Church register, Hamnet was buried there on 11 August 1596. No cause of death is given – plague, still hanging around the country in pockets, was the likely culprit; on the other hand, he was presumably living in Henley Street with his mother, sisters and grandparents, and the household had no other casualties. Even if they survived infancy, one in three children died before reaching their teens in the late 16th century, so Hamnet's death wasn't a rarity, but it must have been a blow. We don't know whether his father attended his funeral – on horseback, London to Stratford was about three days' travel.

'Grief fills the room up of my absent child,
Lies in his bed, walks up and down with me...'

—*King John*, Act 3, Scene 4

In other news, persistent non-attendance had lost John Shakespeare his position on Stratford's council in 1586; by the early '90s he may have recovered a little financially – there are records of several legal actions he took to recover debts over this period – indicating that money was at least owing to him.

Aspiring Gentry

Late in 1596, the Shakespeare family made a second application to be granted a coat of arms. This time, it was successful. On 20 October, for the cost of around £20, they won the right to use the coveted indicator of gentlemanly status – a golden shield with a black diagonal bar, within which was a silver-tipped golden spear. Had John reapplied, or was William the instigator this time? It's tempting to imagine that the son put in the necessary application to cheer his father up, but there's no way to know for sure.

Opposite: View towards Holy Trinity Church, where Hamnet Shakespeare had been baptised in 1585, and where he was buried in 1596.

Below: Shakespeare's coat of arms, on the left drawn in 1602, for a formal listing in *The Book of Coates and Crests*, and on the right shown complete in a modern graphic.

The Lost Letter

'I hope you will have a better conscience… to pay your husbands debte'

—The author of the letter making a direct appeal to 'Mrs Shakspaire's' finer feelings

We've become used to the idea that William and Anne Shakespeare had a remote and probably loveless marriage, so a brand-new theory with evidence to back it comes as a welcome change. Did Anne spend some time living in London?

In 2025, an article was published in the journal of the Shakespeare Society. It was based on research around two fragments of a letter discovered – in the mid-1970s – in the binding of a 17th-century book, but which previously hadn't been studied in detail.

In Shakespeare's time old documents weren't wasted; they were often used to strengthen new bindings. These pieces were found in the binding of a book from the printshop of Richard Field, Shakespeare's old associate from Stratford. The letter is addressed to 'Good Mrs Shakspaire' and raises the interests of a fatherless boy, John Butts, who is coming to the end of his apprenticeship, at which point he is owed money held in trust for him by 'Mrs Shakspaire's' husband. So far, the husband has refused to pay. On the back, in a different handwriting is what seems to be a partial reply, arguing that the letter-writer is the one responsible for the debt. Between them, the fragments contain several names along with an address, Trinity Lane. A lot of academic sleuthing later, the author has gone some way to finding a potential John Butts in London, along with a Trinity Lane originally on the north bank of the Thames. The rarity of the Shakespeare name narrows the list of possible 'Shakspaires' down.

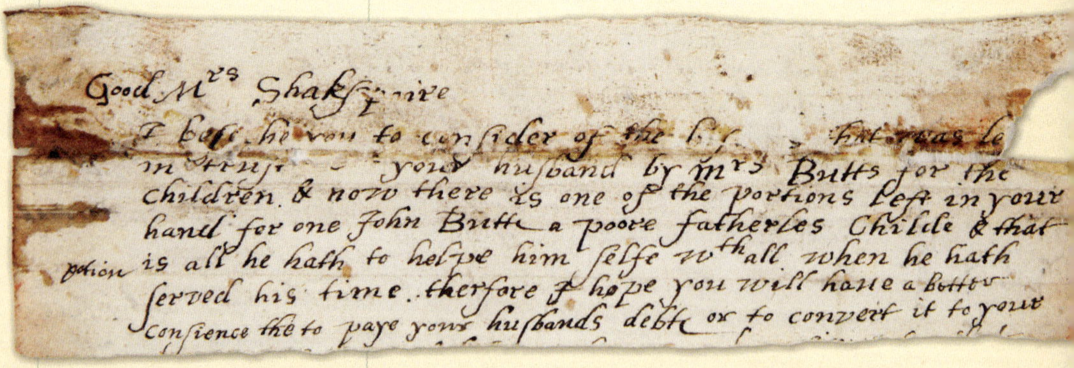

Good Mrs Shakspaire
I [illegible] you to consider of the [illegible]
in trust [illegible] your husband by Mrs Butts for the
children & now there is one of the portions left in your
hand for one John Butts a poore fatherles Childe & that
portion is all he hath to helpe him selfe withall when he hath
served his time therfore I hope you will have a better
Conscience then to paye your husbands debte or to convert it to your

Tracking the Evidence

The connections are complicated, but the author concludes that it's at least a possibility that the Shakespeares lived together in London some of the time during William's long stay there. Does this prove a closer connection between the couple? Not yet. Does it set the scene for more research and further discoveries? Certainly. For any Shakespeare enthusiast, it's an intriguing development. Watch this space.

Opposite top: The only possible likeness we have of Anne Hathaway, this drawing dates from 1708; said to have been traced from a Tudor original, it was labelled 'Shakespeare's consort'.

Opposite bottom: The intriguing letter fragment that sparked the research.

Below: The cosy interior of Anne Hathaway's cottage in Stratford, where it was long believed she spent most of her married life.

The Courting Settle, Anne Hathaway's Cottage.

Acting and Writing

DAY IN THE LIFE
Of course Shakespeare acted as well as writing – the main criticism of the 'upstart crow' of 1592 was that he was an actor turned playwright. Looking at his collected works, though, and knowing something about the daily routine of a company man, you wonder how on earth he managed to juggle his workload.

Shakespeare didn't play leads, but no company members were 'spares', and most would usually have been performing a different play every day of the working week. There is a handful of roles that he is said by near-contemporaries to have taken in his own plays (and of course he'll also have acted in the works of others). It's fairly certain that he played the Ghost in *Hamlet* and Theseus in *A Midsummer Night's Dream*, and possibly Mercutio in *Romeo and Juliet*. These aren't insignificant roles – he may never have had to carry a play on stage, but he must have been versatile as well as able.

The Realities of Writing

As for writing, he must have spent a lot of time working in his various London lodgings, keeping either very late or very early hours, given the other calls on his time. From his friends' elegies after his death, it doesn't sound as though he was ever at a loss

'He...had an excellent fancy, brave notions, and gentle expressions, wherein he flowed with that facility that sometime it was necessary he should be stopped.'

—Ben Jonson remembering the speed and ease with which Shakespeare wrote

for ideas, nor for the words to express them. Working under pressure, though, would have been the norm for all playwrights – with the constant demand for new material, they had to be quick and prolific.

Thomas Heywood, another actor-playwright, who worked with the Admiral's Men, made a notorious boast that he had had 'either an entire hand or at least a maine finger' in 220 plays. Which, even if those collaborations were small ones, makes Shakespeare's known total of 37 plays seem reasonable.

Opposite: An early 19th-century German illustration of one of the most dramatic scenes in *Hamlet*; it's thought Shakespeare himself was the first to play the ghost of Hamlet's father.

Below: An early 20th-century imagining of convivial theatrical society three centuries before.

The Wild Boy

CHRISTOPHER MARLOWE Marlowe was Shakespeare's contemporary – they were born in the same year – and came from a similar background. The son of a Canterbury shoemaker, he attended the town's prestigious King's School, then went on to study at Cambridge, before embarking on a packed but all-too-brief life in London.

He was probably recruited into the secret service, led by the Queen's spymaster Francis Walsingham, while still a student – in his last year at Cambridge he was absent for long periods. The college was persuaded to graduate him on a direct appeal from the Privy Council, claiming that he was working to 'the benefit of his country'. Marlowe was certainly precocious: it's possible that he also wrote the groundbreaking two-parter *Tamburlaine the Great* while still at university, and it was soon followed by *Doctor Faustus*.

An Appetite for Life

Marlowe's writing style was energetic and muscular – at a time when new plays were often stylistically stiff, without much characterisation. *Tamburlaine*, with its easy blank verse, exotic Eastern setting, and magnetic central character, was instantly popular and must have shown Shakespeare that the theatre

Below: Queen Elizabeth with Sir Francis Walsingham, key member of the Privy Council and head of her intelligence service.

Right: Title page of the 1631 edition of *Doctor Faustus*, by then popular for over 40 years.

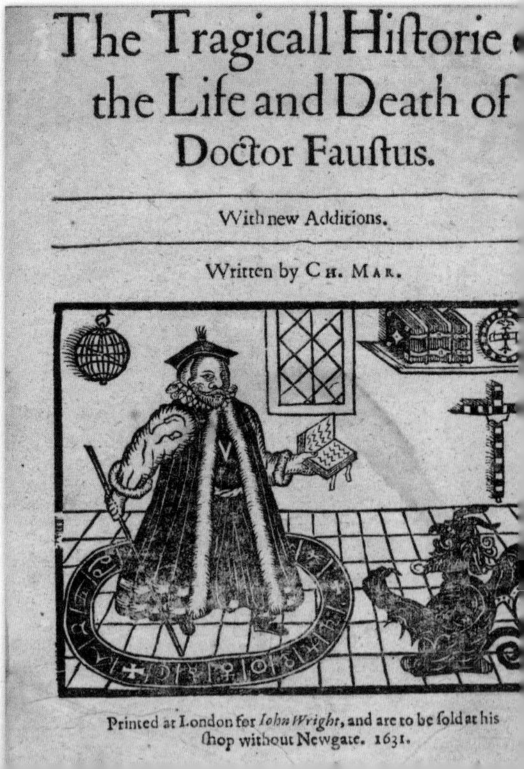
The Tragicall Hiſtorie
the Life and Death of
Doctor Fauſtus.

With new Additions.

Written by CH. MAR.

Printed at London for *Iohn Wright*, and are to be ſold at his ſhop without Newgate. 1631.

could easily accommodate the style he was developing himself. From 1587 Marlowe was in London, where, linked to the Lord Admiral's Men, he wrote plays (new research strengthens claims that he and Shakespeare knew each other well enough to collaborate on all three parts of *Henry VI*) and probably continued to work as an agent. The impression is of someone bursting with energy: an innovator in theatre, he was also an independent thinker – in fact, he was facing charges of atheism when he was killed.

Marlowe's murder in 1593, aged 29, 'stabbed in a tavern in Deptford' (actually lodgings, and most likely a safe house for Walsingham's spies), cut short a career that might plausibly have matched Shakespeare's. As it was, Marlowe wrote seven plays in less than six years, and they remained favourites with the Lord Admiral's Men long after his death.

'Time passeth swift away; Our life is frail, and we may die today.'

—*Tamburlaine the Great*, Part I, Act 1, Scene 1

Below: A late 19th-century painting of Timur the Lame, the 14th-century ruler on whose story Marlowe based *Tamburlaine*.

Friend and Rival

Ben Jonson

If Marlowe was a trailblazer, anticipating some of Shakespeare's own innovations, Ben Jonson, who outlived the older playwright by more than two decades, was perhaps his natural successor as well as his good friend.

Jonson multitasked with a vengeance – his contemporaries knew him as well for his masques as for his plays, and he was also a highly regarded poet.

Fond though he was of Shakespeare, it was clearly a competitive friendship; Jonson criticises the older playwright for his 'Little Latin and less Greek' and snipes about his 'facility', possibly implying that he tends to run on a bit more than strictly necessary.

Right: Jonson, like Shakespeare, came from a relatively modest background, but achieved great success within his lifetime, both with his plays and with the masques he devised for the court.

Opposite top: The demands the stage put on actors meant that many were skilled fencers, as well as accomplished singers and musicians.

Opposite bottom: Men and women acted together in masques, often splendidly and fantastically costumed.

Hard Living

Jonson worked briefly as a bricklayer, like his father, and served as a soldier before he fixed on the theatre for a living. He worked with Pembroke's and the Admiral's Men in the 1590s; of his 18 surviving plays, the satirical *Volpone* is probably best known today. Although posterity has somehow awarded Marlowe the bad-boy reputation, it was Jonson who killed Gabriel Spencer – a fellow actor who was his cellmate when he was jailed for the scandalous *Isle of Dogs* episode – in a duel in 1598. Jonson's knowledge of Latin saved him from the gallows, enabling him to claim 'benefit of clergy', a legal loophole from medieval times, and to get away with a branded thumb. Acting was a risky business: if tempers ran high, your colleagues all had well-practised rapier skills to fall back on.

Art of the Masque

Masques were to become especially popular after the accession of King James – his queen, Anne of Denmark, was a particular enthusiast. More like formalised allegories than plays, they were court entertainments, combining music, dancing and singing, and were often splendidly costumed, with astounding sets. Jonson's collaborations with Inigo Jones, known for his staging skills, were famously magnificent. All the participants were masked, and only some were professionals; theatrically inclined aristocrats took part including, on at least one occasion, Queen Anne herself. Although Shakespeare doesn't appear to have written masques specifically, he wrote masque-like interludes into *A Midsummer Night's Dream* and *The Tempest*.

Young Men About Court

ARISTOCRATS AND PATRONS
Because his two long poems were dedicated to the glamorous young Earl of Southampton, and his sonnets show a passionate engagement to an unidentified young man, also a nobleman, there's long been an interest in Shakespeare's involvement with aristocratic youth.

There's no evidence either way pointing to Shakespeare having gay relationships, although as there's very little solid evidence about his relationships in general, this isn't significant. However, life in the creative arts in Elizabethan and early Jacobean times didn't have any safety nets, and having important allies working in your interest, whether or not they were formal patrons, was crucial. And while Shakespeare was a great artist, he was also, in the manner of the times, an outrageous flatterer, reflecting a glorious vision of themselves back to his patrons.

What role did the patrons see themselves playing? An interest in the arts would have been educated into many young aristocrats and, as always, those with time and money to invest used them in service of their artistic and charitable interests. For the younger Shakespeare, attracting the Earl of Southampton – one of the richest men in England – as a patron was a coup.

Left: Henry Wriothesley, Earl of Southampton, around 1603, in full court finery.

Opposite top: James I would prove to be a dedicated patron of the theatre.

Opposite bottom: Formal dress for rich young men in the 1590s and 1600s was as extravagant and colourful as that for women.

'My Lord of Southampton and Lord Rutland come not to Court... They pass away the time in London merely in going to plays every day.'

—Rowland Whyte to his employer, Robert Sydney, Earl of Leicester, 1599

And he would rise higher; eventually his company would enjoy the patronage of the King himself. Was there a closer relationship with Southampton or others? We can't know, but it seems wildly unlikely: a busy playwright with aspirations to a rather bourgeois gentry and a member of the aristocracy with his own fish to fry at court seem an unlikely romantic pairing.

The Appeal of the Theatre

The theatre was highly fashionable, but that didn't eliminate class distinctions – the actors, after all, were even costumed in the aristocracy's cast-offs. Sometimes such distinctions were overcome by intellectual interests, but most often when young aristocrats visited the theatres, rather than attending court performances, part of the enjoyment would have been that they were consciously slumming it.

'To the Onlie Begetter...'

SHAKESPEARE'S SONNETS
Even readers who aren't particular enthusiasts know Shakespeare's sonnets better than they think. There are 154 of them, and dozens of lines and stanzas from them have entered everyday language to the point at which their origin is almost forgotten.

This probably hasn't done them any favours with the reading public. Repeat any line/s of poetry often enough, even when they're belters, like 'Love is not love/which alters when it alteration finds', and they start to sound banal. But Shakespeare's sonnets are beautiful, original – and baffling. Although there's no indication that they were written for anything other than personal pleasure – perhaps to be shared with friends – luckily for us, they were printed as a collection in 1609, under unclear circumstances: we don't know whether it was with Shakespeare's permission or not.

Scholars think it's likely that they were written over a long period, stretching from the early 1590s to close to the date they were published. Their 'onlie begetter' dedication 'To Mr W H' has been pored over and examined without any candidate ever being convincingly confirmed. The poems' storyline has kept academics puzzling for the last 400 years: is Shakespeare confiding in the reader about a homosexual passion? Were some sonnets commissioned to try to persuade a young aristocrat into marriage? What does the Dark Lady have on Shakespeare, and was she a real person (there are at least five candidates)? An in-depth look is too big a demand for a small book, so on the page opposite is a short rundown. It is, though, well worth reading them for yourself.

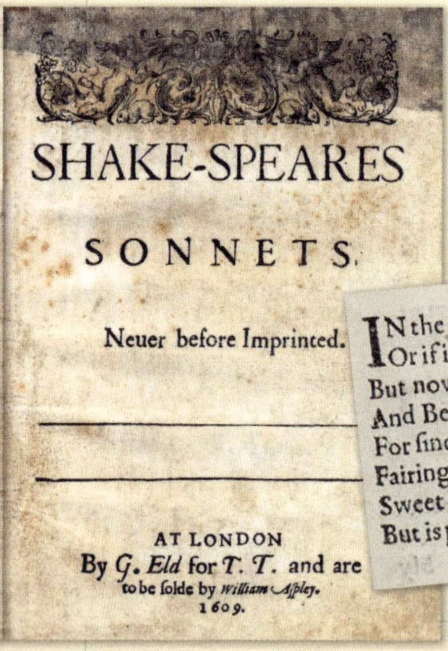
SHAKE-SPEARES

SONNETS.

Neuer before Imprinted.

AT LONDON
By G. Eld for T. T. and are
to be solde by William Aspley.
1609.

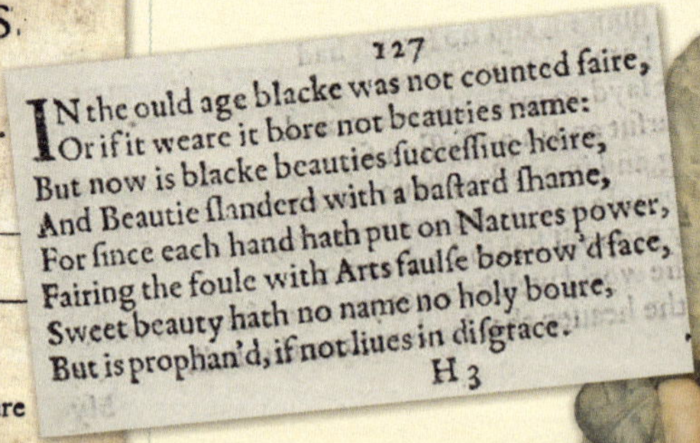
127

IN the ould age blacke was not counted faire,
Or if it weare it bore not beauties name:
But now is blacke beauties ſucceſſiue heire,
And Beautie ſlanderd with a baſtard ſhame,
For ſince each hand hath put on Natures power,
Fairing the foule with Arts faulſe borrow'd face,
Sweet beauty hath no name no holy boure,
But is prophan'd, if not liues in diſgrace.

H 3

Sonnet Basics

- **Shakespeare sticks to his sonnet formula – three four-line verses, each with different rhyme pairings (ABAB, CDCD, EFEF), finished with a rhyming couplet (GG) which sometimes contains a twist.**
- **The traditional scholarly view is that the sonnets fall into three groups – numbers 1 to 126 are addressed to a beautiful and probably aristocratic youth with whom the poet seems to be in love, and all the dramas that come out of the uneven relationship.**
- **Numbers 127 to 152 are addressed to a dark lady, who is the poet's lover, but whom he depicts unconventionally – she's not young, she's not beautiful, her behaviour is awful, but he's still obsessed with her.**
- **Numbers 153 and 154 are the odd ones out; they're about Cupid and Psyche.**
- **Believing the Beautiful Youth and the Dark Lady were real people in Shakespeare's life, readers have longed to identify them – there are whole books on the subject. Slightly less popular is the theory that he may have confected characters to create persuasive fictions, just as in his plays, but this time for his own pleasure.**

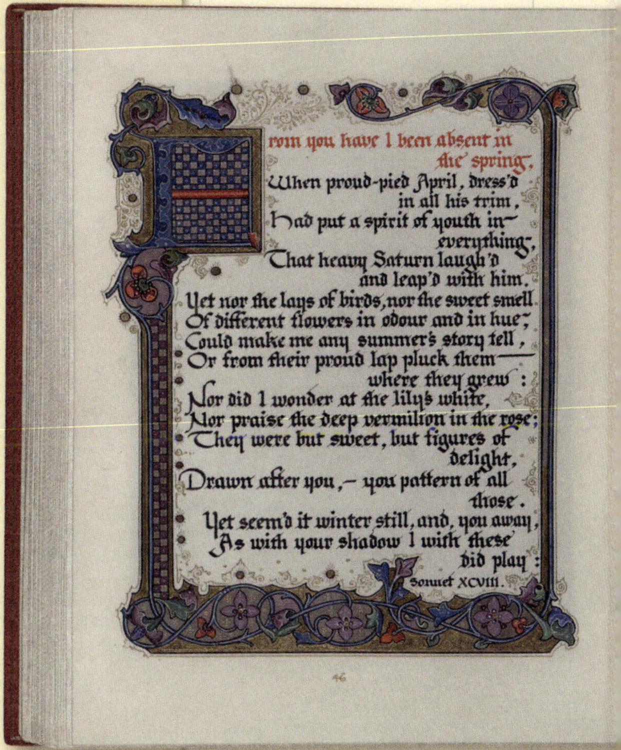

Opposite left: Title page of the first published collection, from 1609, and one of the Dark Lady sonnets, 127, from inside.

Opposite right: Mary Fitton, one of Elizabeth's maids of honour – and one of several candidates considered for the Dark Lady role.

Above: Sonnet 98, from an illuminated collection created to mark the three-century anniversary of their first publication.

Making Money

Taking Care of Business
There was one aspect of many fellow actors and playwrights that Shakespeare doesn't seem to have shared: there's no indication that he was ever a hellraiser. Where he does crop up in official documents, it's mostly because he's bought some property or defaulted on his tax.

By comparison with Marlowe, Jonson, Kyd, Greene and others, Shakespeare seems to have been the sensible one. He worked hard and there are no records of major fallings-out with colleagues. From a jobbing actor and writer, he graduated first to a sharer in his company and ultimately, at the Globe, to a shareholder in his theatre (known as a housekeeper). And as he earned, he seems to have invested.

A Prudent Investor

We know that in 1596, it was probably William who had paid the £20 for a family coat of arms; in the following year he began a move into property, swapping the family home – adequate but not grand – for New Place, 'the second-largest house in Stratford' in the centre of town, with its imposing bays overlooking Chapel

Sam. Ireland. del.

Shakspere's House, New Place, Chapel, & Grammar School.

Street. It offered plenty of space to support the extended family in style. The purchase documents show that it cost him £60. In 1602, he bought a plot of 107 acres, again near Stratford, and in 1605, he was to make an investment in the tithes, compulsory taxes all citizens paid to the church, which should have repaid itself well within a year or two.

None of these investments were extravagant: they complete our picture of Shakespeare as a canny money manager who didn't take risks and who kept his funds close to home. However well he did in the theatre – and scholars estimate that he might have earned a handsome £200 in a good year – it would never be a stable profession. After all, when plague broke out in London it could close the theatres overnight, for months. Shakespeare remained careful.

'Money buys lands, and wives are sold by fate.'

—*The Merry Wives of Windsor*, Act 5, Scene 5

Opposite: New Place, the Shakespeares' grand new home, had been built by Hugh Clopton (also responsible for the Clopton Bridge) in the 1480s. Sadly, it was demolished in the mid-18th century.

Below: *The Rent Collectors*, painted in 1618 by Pieter Brueghel the Younger, illustrating the gathering of the tithes in the Netherlands. Shakespeare's investment in a share of the local tithes collected in Stratford would have helped to ensure a steady income for his family.

Build it Back Up

BIRTH OF THE GLOBE
In 1598, the long-term disagreements the Burbages had with their Puritan landlord Giles Allen seem to have come to a head. Allen made it clear to the Lord Chamberlain's Men that he did not intend to renew the lease on the site of The Theatre.

James Burbage had made a hash of things. In 1596 he had started to convert some rundown upper rooms in a building on the site of the old monastery at Blackfriars into a new theatre – one with a roof, which would have meant the company could perform in any weather. Midway through the conversion, the neighbours objected – theatres, after all, tended to be indicators of a rackety neighbourhood – and further work on the building was stopped. James died at the beginning of 1597 (his management role would be largely taken over by his sons, especially the elder, Cuthbert, who did not act), and the Burbage brothers made a pragmatic decision. The Theatre was simply going to have to accompany them to a new site. In December, the building was dismantled overnight and the materials carried from Shoreditch into storage.

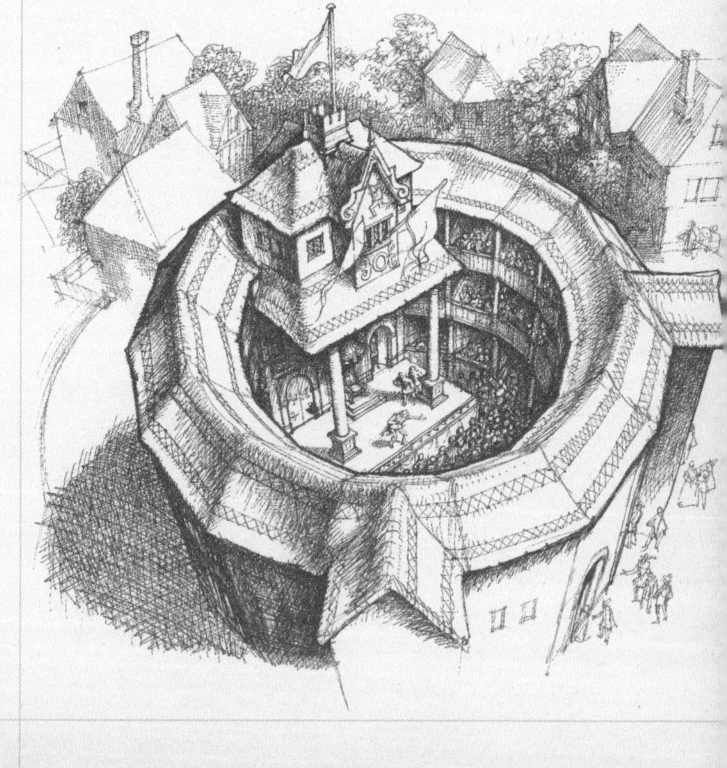

Right: An aerial reconstruction of the Globe, showing the thatched roof covering the good seats, and the open stage.

Opposite: The Globe, with the Rose shown in the background. The raised flags indicated the kind of play being staged: a black flag for tragedy, white for comedy and red for a history.

The Burbages had found a new site in Southwark, on the south bank of the Thames, close to the Rose, and had negotiated a long lease with a complaisant landlord. The theatre they would build with the reclaimed timbers was called the Globe. It opened in the spring of 1599, probably with an inaugural performance of Shakespeare's *Julius Caesar*.

A New Kind of Management

To cope financially, the Burbage sons made a new agreement with the other sharers in the Lord Chamberlain's Men: if they contributed to the construction costs of the Globe, they would be rewarded with a share in the theatre as well as the company. If things went well with the new theatre, this offered the possibility that they might become rich men.

'There is a tide in the affairs of men, Which, taken at the flood, leads on to fortune...'

—*Julius Caesar*, Act 4, Scene 3

Shakespeare's Funny Men

A Change of Parts
Will Kempe had been the star comedian with the Lord Chamberlain's Men since their formation; he had been as solid a part of their line-up as Richard Burbage. But in 1599, for reasons that can't be pinned down, he left the company.

Kempe seems to have been gradually pushed out, and when he left, pledging to dance his way out of the world – a pun on the Globe – all the way to Norwich, he wasn't on good terms with the other members. Shakespeare scholars have noted the repudiation of Sir John Falstaff – most likely a Kempe-created role, and a hugely successful one – in his plays and wonder if life had somehow mirrored art.

From Clown to Fool

The company still needed a lead comic, and Kempe's replacement was a very different character. Robert Armin, who joined the company as an actor and sharer in 1600, was a skilled musician and a comic writer of ballads and poems – in many ways a more modern man than Kempe, with his jigs, traditional slapstick and

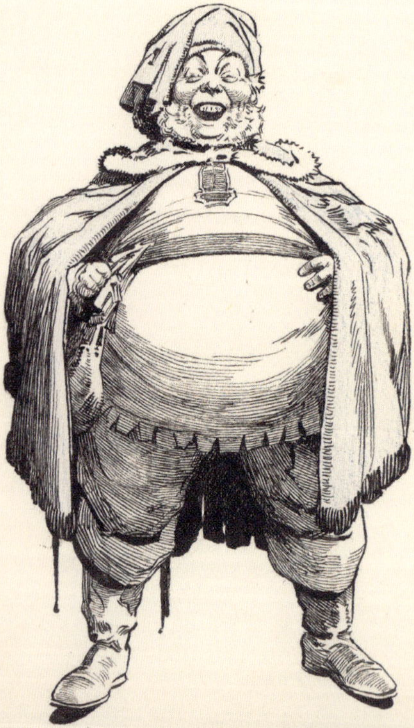

THE
Hiſtory of the two Maids of More-clacke,
VVith the life and ſimple maner of IOHN
in the Hoſpitall.
Played by the Children of the Kings
Maieſties Reuels.
VVritten by ROBERT ARMIN, ſeruant to the Kings
moſt excellent Maieſtie.

LONDON,
Printed by *N.O.* for *Thomas Archer*, and is to be ſold at his
ſhop in Popes-head Pallace, 1609.

copious ad libs, could ever have been. Once he was working with Armin, Shakespeare's fools change: they become more complex, wiser and sometimes darker, too. Kempe had made a hilarious Bottom in *A Midsummer Night's Dream*; evidently, he excelled at rustic, unselfconsciously funny simpletons. Armin, on the other hand, would play Touchstone in *As You Like It*, and Feste in *Twelfth Night*; ultimately, he would become the philosopher-fool of *King Lear*.

These parts place less emphasis on broad physical comedy, instead offering subtler insights on a play's action. The question is, was Shakespeare sick of obvious clowning, and yearning to write these more complex parts during Kempe's time, or was he, like any good company playwright, simply adjusting to the arrival of Armin and working to his troupe's strengths?

Opposite left: The tumultuous, overbearing character of Falstaff may have been created for Will Kempe.

Opposite right: The title page of a play written by Robert Armin, an author as well as a talented comic, for the Children of the King's Revels.

Below: Shakespeare's comic roles vary from broad, physical knockabout – such as Bottom, seen here charming Titania with his ass's head – to subtler roles like Touchstone in *As You Like It*, or Feste in *Twelfth Night*.

'And let those that play your clowns speak no more than is set down for them, for there be of them that will themselves laugh...'

—*Hamlet*, Act 3, Scene 2

Hamlet

*'This above all:
to thine own
self be true,
And it must follow,
as the night the day
Thou canst not
then be false to
any man.'*

—*Hamlet*, Act 1, Scene 3

If there's a quintessential Shakespearean play that encapsulates all his strengths, shows him at the top of his form, and leaves every audience feeling it was both revelatory and familiar, it's probably *Hamlet*. Almost everyone can quote from it, even if they've never actually seen it performed.

What is it about this particular play, with its anguished central protagonist? As was so often the case, Shakespeare didn't invent the story: the original tale of 'Amleth' is found in a 12th-century history of Denmark, *Gesta Danorum*, and retold in the French *Histoires Tragiques* by Francois de Belleforest, published in 1570. Even closer to home, Thomas Kyd had written another Hamlet – a lost version, which has since become known to scholars as the Ur-Hamlet – which was performed in the late 1580s. We can't know how close the story was to Shakespeare's, as no printed copy survives.

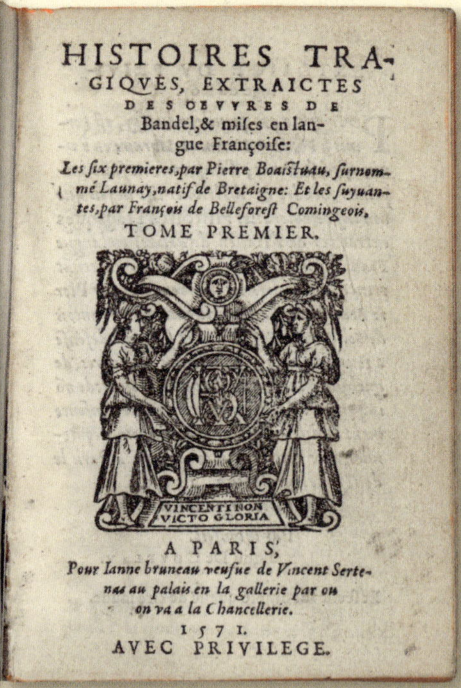

HISTOIRES TRAGIQVES, EXTRAICTES DES OEVVRES DE Bandel,& miſes en langue Françoiſe:

Les ſix premieres,par Pierre Boaiſtuau, ſurnommé Launay,natif de Bretaigne: Et les ſuyuantes,par François de Belleforeſt Comingeois,

TOME PREMIER.

A PARIS,

Pour Ianne bruneau veufue de Vincent Sertenas au palais en la gallerie par ou on va a la Chancellerie.

1571.

AVEC PRIVILEGE.

Opposite: A woodcut from the source work for *Hamlet*, *Gesta Danorum*, alongside the title page of its French retelling, de Belleforest's *Histoires Tragiques*.

Left: Act 5, scene 1, illustrated here, combines the comedy of the gravediggers with one of Hamlet's best-known speeches, prompted by Yorick's unearthed skull.

A Modern Hero

So, Shakespeare uses magpie skills to create a complicated revenge tragedy. Hamlet, the longest part he ever wrote, becomes an everyman figure; the Danish prince, within his web of regicide, plotting and endless unsolvable dilemmas, has proved adaptable to any culture or time. Compared with earlier works, Shakespeare's characterisation is so real, his prince so conscious and the plot so involving, that the play marks a new stage in his work. The idea of distinctive individuality was a relatively new one in the late 16th century, when conformity was desirable, but Shakespeare embraced it without hesitation.

Richard Burbage was Shakespeare's first Hamlet. The role cemented his widespread star status, even though in 1601 when it was probably first staged, he was in his mid-30s – well into middle age – and putting on weight. The audience didn't care: both player and play were a hit.

Twelfth Night

THE MATURE COMEDY
Named for the celebration that traditionally brought each year's Christmas festivities to a close, *Twelfth Night* gets its first mention from John Manningham, a student of Middle Temple, who was in the audience when it was staged in the palatial Middle Temple Hall on Candlemas, 2 February 1602.

This private performance for lawyers is unlikely to have been *Twelfth Night*'s first; the Lord Chamberlain's Men had probably given the new play a debut on home turf at the Globe. It's often considered to be Shakespeare's most polished comedy, one in which he takes ingredients he's already practised with and uses them to cook up an accomplished recipe of aristocratic manners, ironic humour, broad comedy and some extremely complicated reflections on the nature of attraction and love.

Familiar Surroundings

Nominally, the play is set in Illyria (probably present-day Croatia), but despite the implied 'foreignness' of the surroundings, the manners and habits are comfortingly familiar; there are the households of the aristocracy, and the less refined situations of coarser relations and underlings. Initiated, not for the only time in Shakespeare's works, by a shipwreck, the action delivers a complex lovers' knot based on misunderstandings, cross-dressing and the familiar conceit of identical twins – this time one male, one female – which neatly unravels into three satisfactory marriages – two more-or-less romantic, one comic – and everybody having learned a few lessons along the way.

Opposite: On the left, Middle Temple Hall, which saw *Twelfth Night*'s first known performance and on the right, an illustration of Malvolio's attempt to please, complete with yellow cross-gartering.

Left: *Twelfth Night*, Act 5, scene 1, in which the carefully manufactured confusion of the plot finally starts to unravel.

Below: Feste, the attendant fool – and observant commentator – of Olivia's household.

'Cesario, come –
For so you shall be, while you are a man.
But when in other habits you are seen,
Orsino's mistress, and his fancy's queen.'

—*Twelfth Night*, Act 5, Scene 1

In Feste, the fool of Olivia's household, Shakespeare has written his first 'mature' jester, presumably to be performed by Robert Armin – 'better a witty fool than a foolish wit'; also, taking account of his new actor's musicality, he has included several songs. Broader comedy hasn't been abandoned, just reined in a little: a riotous subplot conspires to puncture the tragic self-importance of Olivia's pompous household steward, Malvolio (who, it's been suggested, may have been played by Shakespeare himself). It's all thoroughly satisfying.

The King's Men

The End of an Era
In March 1603, Elizabeth I died. Her reign had lasted for 44 years and she had retained her status as Virgin Queen until the end, only grudgingly accepting – never having named him – that her successor would be the son of Mary Queen of Scots, James VI of Scotland.

James had been ruler of Scotland from infancy, when his mother was deposed. He was 36 when he took the English throne, and posterity gives him mixed reviews. However, whatever his political or personal qualities, he was certainly a supporter of theatre, as was his wife, Anne of Denmark. He arrived in England a couple of months after Elizabeth's death, and on 18 May he placed the Lord Chamberlain's Men under royal patronage, renaming them the King's Men. They were given fine red cloth to make liveries, and honorary titles – the company members became Grooms of the King's Bedchamber.

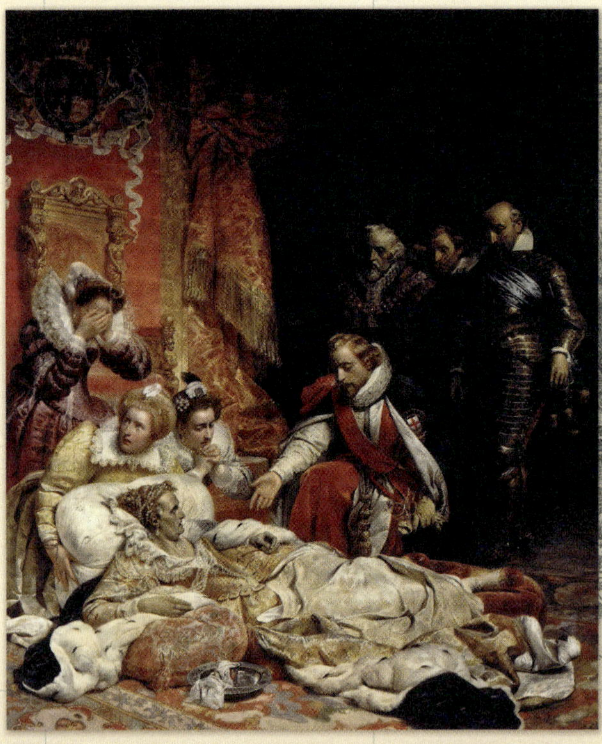

First Impressions

By the time the new king arrived in the south, London was, yet again, in the throes of a bad plague season, and the theatres had to be closed. In any case, he shortly left the capital to make a progress around the provinces, over the next few months staying on several occasions at Wilton, home of the Earl of Pembroke, near Salisbury. It's believed that it was at Wilton, early in December 1603, that the King's Men first entertained James, probably with a performance of *As You Like It*. They were paid £30, considered generous, although it's unclear if it was James or his host, the Earl, who stumped up. Over Christmas they would perform again for the King, this time at Hampton Court.

Opposite left: Elizabeth I died slowly, declining over many days, as shown in this dramatic painting of 1828 by Paul Delaroche.

Opposite right: James I of England, and VI of Scotland, shown with his queen, Anne of Denmark, in a contemporary engraving.

Below: The celebrated early 19th-century comic actor John Pritt Harley, shown in the role of Touchstone in *As You Like It*.

> 'His honour and the greatness of his name
> Shall be, and make new nations: he shall flourish,
> And, like a mountain cedar, reach his branches
> To all the plains about him...'

—*Henry VIII*, Act 5, Scene 4

CHAPTER FOUR

THE FOREMOST MAKER

'London, plaguey London...'

The Theatres Close Again

When plague closed the London theatres shortly after King James's accession, it was the start of a difficult few years for Londoners. 'London, plaguey London, full of danger and vice', wrote the poet John Donne in 1607, and many of his contemporaries would have agreed.

Plague came in waves and hit the capital most summers, but from 1603 there was a run of particularly bad seasons. In 1604 the Privy Council issued a decree that if plague was the cause of 30 or more deaths per week in London, theatres and other places of entertainment must shut until the death toll fell.

Back on Tour

Application of the Council's rule seems to have been a bit hit-or-miss, but it prompted acting companies to tour the provinces – provincial stagings may have paid less generously, but at least they paid something. The King himself encouraged the King's Men to tour, believing that they were good ambassadors for the monarchy.

We don't know whether Shakespeare always accompanied them, though it seems likely that he went on at least some tours. The list of productions they offered was certainly impressive – when the theatres closed for the umpteenth time towards the end of July 1606, the plays of that season – soon to be shown in Oxford, Ipswich and elsewhere – included Shakespeare's *Macbeth* and *King Lear* (at 42, he was hitting the peak of his powers), Jonson's *Volpone*, and Thomas Middleton's brand-new and highly fashionable *Revenger's Tragedy*.

Left: In a bad year, there might be nobody left who was prepared to dispose of the bodies of those who had died from plague.

Below: A panorama of London made in around 1600 by the Dutch engraver Claes Visscher. By the start of the 17th century it had a (then immense) population of around 200,000. Plague travelled quickly in its cramped streets.

The tours may have been great for the county towns, but scholars have estimated that between 1606 and 1610 the London theatres were only able to open for nine months in total – overall, very bad for business. In October 1606, with the King's Men still on tour, back in London plague came close to home when it killed Mrs Mountjoy, Shakespeare's Huguenot landlady.

'Thou art a boil, a plague sore, an embossed carbuncle in my corrupted blood.'

—*King Lear*, Act 2, Scene 4

Theatre Flops

A Notable Failure

The record of how new plays were received in Elizabethan or Jacobean theatre is spotty: usually only repeat performances, widespread pirating or imitation tell you that a play was successful. Unsuccessful plays tended simply to disappear.

There's an exception, though, for the 1603 debut of Ben Jonson's *Sejanus* at the Globe. The play was not a success and the performance ended in a rout. How do we know? Unusually, four separate contemporary or near-contemporary accounts tell us so. If a play was unpopular at court, it fell quietly out of the repertoire; in public performance, a rowdier audience was freer with its opinion.

'I, amongst others, hissed Sejanus off the stage…'

—The essayist Francis Osborne, recalls being in the audience, aged nine, for that first performance

Taken from Tacitus, *Sejanus*, the story of the ambitious favourite of the Emperor Tiberius, who overreaches and is eventually torn to pieces by the Roman mob, was very long and crammed with ambitious speeches. Even with Richard Burbage in the title role and William Shakespeare (probably) playing Tiberius, it failed to engage the audience. Shouts were followed by missiles, and the actors were, if not torn to pieces, at least heckled off the stage by a real-life mob.

Later, in the dedication to his patron of the printed play, Jonson would claim that the fault lay not with Sejanus but with an audience that was too unsophisticated to appreciate it: pearls before swine, in fact. Staged in 2005, in a revival by the Royal Shakespeare Company, *Sejanus* was heavily cut.

Opposite left: A scene from *Sejanus*, in which the treacherous general appears to save the Emperor's life.

Opposite right: The theatre audience in Shakespeare's time was close enough to the actors to express any displeasure physically.

Below: Iago, the character *Sejanus* may have inspired Shakespeare to create.

Waste Not, Want Not

Recently, scholars have singled out clear parallels between some aspects of *Sejanus* and *Othello*, and wondered if Shakespeare, ever on the lookout for new ingredients, characteristically reused, in Iago, the idea of an ill-intentioned employee who manipulates his master, with disastrous consequences. They point to similar word play and phrasing. If correct, it's another example of the way in which Shakespeare, even if in this case he was smarting from an acting failure, made sure that nothing ever went to waste.

Inside the Company

SHARERS, ACTORS AND APPRENTICES

What was it like to be a member of the King's Men? The relationships must have been close – whatever your standing within the company, you had a day-to-day responsibility to keep everything running smoothly.

Over time, some players inevitably left, apprentices might be promoted to actors elsewhere and there were some fallings-out (although the fact that the departure of Will Kempe is so well-documented argues that there may not have been very many).

Without diaries or private letters, we can't hear the actors' own voices, but we catch an echo of them in *The Malcontent*, a play originally written by John Marston for the Children of the Chapel, a boy's company. When, in 1604, the King's Men added it to their repertoire, they commissioned a new induction – a sort of satirical preface. Uniquely, it stars three of the company's actors, Richard Burbage, Henry Condell and John Lowin, playing themselves. Two other actors, as their foils, act members of the audience. It's a short piece, but

it gives the actors the chance to ham it up. They make rude jokes, they express their own opinions on the play – generally, they indulge in the sort of smart, self-referential comedy that we think of as highly contemporary now. The audience, of course, are in on the joke. It's the sort of performance that only works with a tight team.

Playing Women

We know Shakespeare had to work to the company strengths – and he surely must have thought ahead to casting, in particular, which of his younger actors or apprentices could play an important woman's part convincingly. Sadly, the information for this area is particularly thin, and we're unlikely ever to know who became the first Juliet, say, or Cleopatra.

'Nay, faith, let me not play a woman; I have a beard coming.'

—*A Midsummer Night's Dream*, Act 1, Scene 2

Opposite left: Engraving of John Lowin, a senior member of the King's Men who would manage the company between 1623 and 1642, when it was closed with the outbreak of war.

Opposite right: Title page of *The Malcontent*, the play whose induction piece gives us our only personal glimpse of the personalities in the company.

Left: Shakespeare never led the King's Men, but he seems to have been an accomplished team player.

Play Setting

OTHER LANDS AND TIMES
As far as we know, Shakespeare never travelled outside England. How did he manage to convey other countries convincingly? And how knowledgeable would his audience have been?

Of course, the plays must be seen through the lens of their time. People wanted to be entertained by a play; a high degree of historical or geographical accuracy wouldn't have been expected, although performances for the King or the courts of law would have had a more educated audience, and a specially written prologue or epilogue, or both, could be used to make the playwright's excuses if thought necessary.

Sources might include a story from the classics; a collection of short stories, a work of history, or even a poem or an earlier play. For his later work, Shakespeare also drew on travellers' tales. Contemporary plays weren't yet seen as enduring pieces of literature, and weren't treated with reverence. They could be reused as they were, or cut-and-pasted into new forms at will.

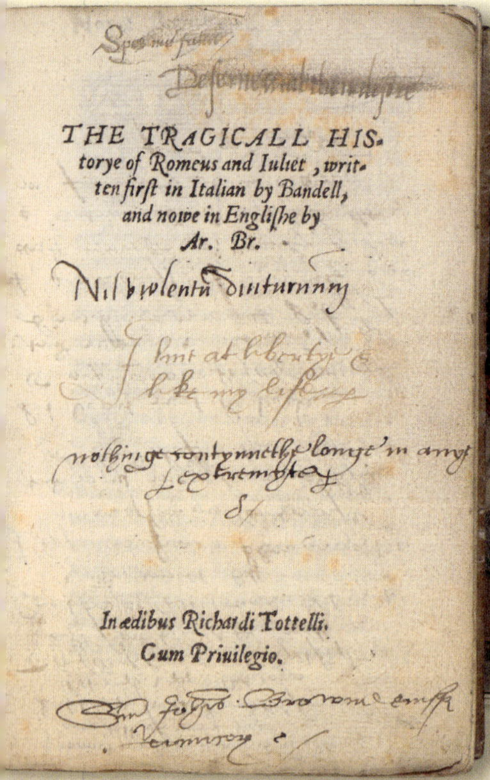
THE TRAGICALL HIStorye of Romeus and Iuliet, writtenfirst in Italian by Bandell, and nowe in Englishe by Ar. Br.

In ædibus Richardi Tottelli.
Cum Priuilegio.

Which Plot From Which Source?

We can track at least some references for most of Shakespeare's plays. *The Tempest* and *Love's Labour's Lost* are two for which he seems to have invented the plots, and *The Merry Wives of Windsor* is self-invention, too, although it has been neatly slotted in with the history plays. Sometimes, references might be in translation; others might call on his knowledge of Latin, French or Italian. Shakespeare never stuck to even detailed sources slavishly.

Known sources include:

- **For *Romeo and Juliet*: *The Tragical History of Romeus and Juliet*, 1562, by the English poet Arthur Brooke.**
- **For *Julius Caesar*, *Antony and Cleopatra*, *Coriolanus* and *Timon of Athens*: *The Lives of the Noble Grecians and Romans*, a 1579 translation of Plutarch's work by Sir Thomas North.**
- **For *All's Well That Ends Well*, *The Two Gentlemen of Verona* and (part of) *Cymbeline*: *The Decameron*, Giovanni Boccaccio's story collection, c.1350.**
- **For *Henry IV*, *Henry V*, *Henry VI*, *Henry VIII*, *Richard II*, *Richard III*, *King Lear*, *Macbeth* and (part of) *Cymbeline*: Holinshed's *Chronicles*, Raphael Holinshed, 1577.**
- **For *Hamlet*: *Gesta Danorum*, Saxo Grammaticus, c.1200.**

THE LIVES
OF THE NOBLE GRE-
CIANS AND ROMANES, COMPARED
together by that graue learned Philosopher and Historiogra-
pher, Plutarke of Chæronea:

Translated out of Greeke into French by IAMES AMYOT, Abbot of Bellozane,
Bishop of Auxerre, one of the Kings priuy counsel, and great Amner
of Fraunce, and out of French into Englishe, by
Thomas North.

Imprinted at London by Thomas Vautroullier dvvelling
in the Blacke Friers by Ludgate.
1579.

Opposite: Title page of an early source for the story of *Romeo and Juliet*, alongside a 19th-century lithograph of Act 3, Scene 5, the morning after.

Above: An engraved portrait of Plutarch above the title page of the North translation that was Shakespeare's source.

Macbeth

The Scottish Play

Although *Macbeth* didn't make it into print before the First Folio in 1623, it probably made its stage debut in 1606 as part of the King's Christmas festivities at Hampton Court. Fast-moving and gruesome, it also appealed to some of James's particular interests.

Catching Royal Attention

First, the witches: everybody knew the King was obsessed with witchcraft. He had conducted witch trials in 1590 in Berwick after a series of violent storms had disrupted his and his new Queen's voyage from Denmark, on the grounds that local witches had raised the tempests. In 1597 he'd even authored *Daemonologie*, a treatise against witchcraft. Macbeth's malign witches not only foretell the future, but in doing so propel Macbeth, Scotland's military hero, into regicide.

Second, King Malcolm's murder. Fear of assassination would have been on James's mind from childhood – his father, Lord Darnley, had been murdered, and Queen Elizabeth had had his mother beheaded; there was plenty of violence in his past. In 1605 the Gunpowder Plot to blow up Parliament had been uncovered and would also have been fresh in the King's mind.

Finally, James claimed a direct lineage back to Banquo – like Macbeth, a figure from 11th-century Scottish history – so the ghostly line-up of future kings and the appearance of Banquo's ghost would not only have been exciting bits of stagecraft but also clear references to his heritage. Shakespeare's source for the plot (he used it for most of his history plays) was Holinshed's *Chronicles*, a history of the British Isles published in 1587. Holinshed describes Banquo as a co-conspirator in Malcolm's murder, but here the playwright made a tactful alteration.

Having outraged the natural order of things with the murder of the king, the Macbeths aren't strong enough to deal with what they've unleashed; inevitably they break. No wonder the new play, if not exactly festive, was a great hit, both at court and, later, when it was staged at the Globe.

'Yet do I fear thy nature. It is too full o'th' milk of human kindness'

—*Macbeth*, Act 1, Scene 5

Opposite: A 19th-century imagining of the witches' raising of gory visions, from Act 4, Scene 1.

Above: Act 3, Scene 4, in which Macbeth – and Macbeth alone – sees Banquo's ghost.

Below: The conspirators behind the Gunpowder Plot. On its discovery, some died fighting, others survived to be executed.

A New Theatre at Blackfriars

A Change of Use
For some time after James Burbage had been refused permission for his company theatre in Blackfriars, the building was used for performances by children's troupes, in particular, the Children of the Chapel Royal.

Boy performers were more desirable neighbours than adult companies. They performed only a couple of times a week (less disruptive to residents), and their stagings were seen as more refined. After James I's accession, the Chapel company came under royal patronage and were renamed the Children of the Queen's Revels. Tactlessly satirical play selections, however (including one in which all the young actors were said to have performed with cod Scottish accents), put them out of favour again. From 1608, Richard and Cuthbert Burbage took over the theatre and Blackfriars became what their father had intended: an all-weather performance space for the King's Men.

'There is daily so great resort of people, and so great multitude of coaches, whereof many are hackney coaches bringing people of all sorts, that sometimes all their streets cannot contain them...'

—Blackfriars Theatre, a victim of its own success, causing traffic jams. Here, the Lord Mayor of London acknowledges the problem, answering residents' complaints in 1619

Comfortable Quarters

Compared with the Globe, Blackfriars was luxurious. It was the first theatre sited inside the London city walls in a salubrious residential area, rather than a disreputable suburb. Entry cost sixpence; the best seats were an extortionate two shillings more. Those keen to see the action up close could buy a seat at the edge of the stage. There were excellent musical accompaniments, too; rather than relying on the instrumental abilities of individual actors, the theatre had its own musicians on call. Evening performances, lit by candlelight, must have been much more atmospheric for, say, a staging of *Macbeth* or *Othello*, than a rainy afternoon at the Globe.

It was here that new plays from the most popular playwrights first appeared, including works from Beaumont and Fletcher – Fletcher was shortly to build an even closer relationship with the King's Men.

Opposite: The Children of the Chapel Royal, centre, playing their part in Elizabeth I's funeral procession.

Below: This side-by-side comparison shows the huge advantages that the new indoor theatres, although much more expensive, would have had for their audiences over the old, Globe or Rose, model.

Modern Habits

SPECIAL EFFECTS
Performances at Blackfriars marked the start of a new kind of theatre in London. Even though the nature of the plays performed didn't immediately change – and the open-air theatres would last a while longer – the opportunities that arrived with a different sort of building offered new possibilities for playwrights, too.

Blackfriars also heralded the arrival of smaller theatres. Its audience capacity was around 700 people, as opposed to the 2,000-plus that could be crammed into the Globe. Nor did this new indoor theatre have standing room – no more groundlings. Its situation, surrounded by a well-to-do neighbourhood, marked a visit out as a more genteel experience.

A New Theatre District

Other theatre men weren't slow to notice the advantages of the Burbages' new space; by 1616 the impresario Christopher Beeston, possibly with the help of Inigo Jones, had converted an old cockfighting arena into the indoor Cockpit Theatre, the first in Drury Lane, in what would eventually become London's theatre district. (After it burned down a year later, he put it up again and rechristened it the Phoenix.) More indoor theatres would follow.

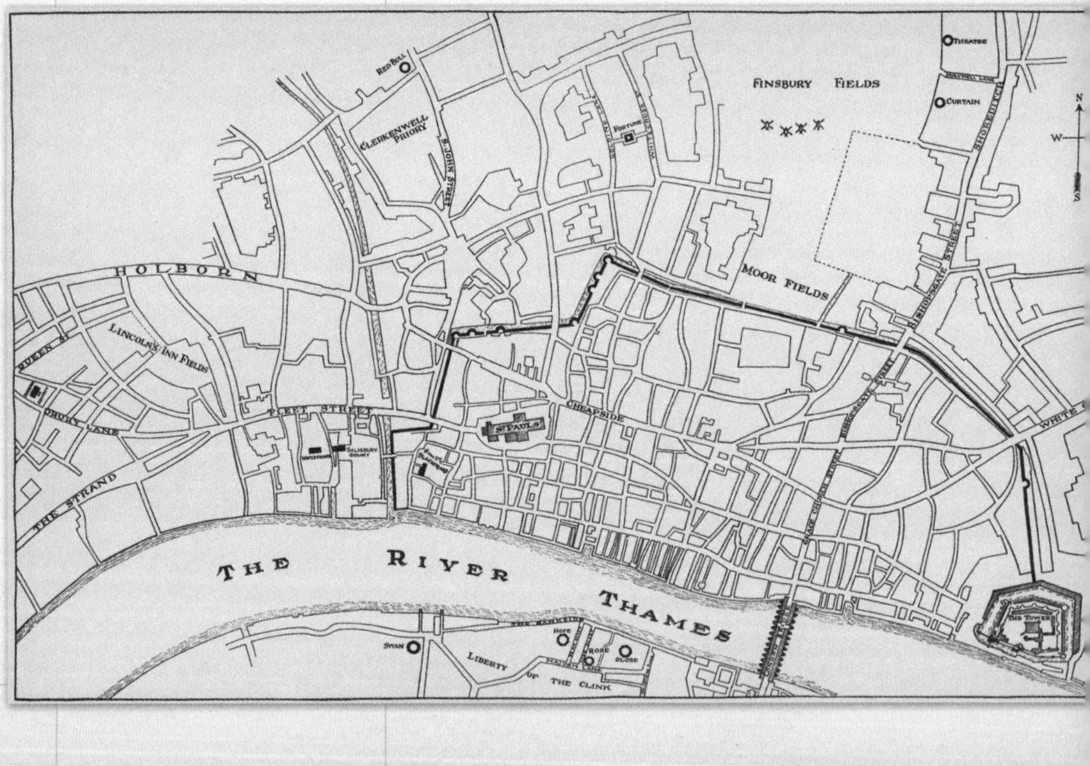

Innovations

As stagings moved indoors, into ever-more custom-built spaces, theatre visits started to change. Jacobean novelties included:

- **Plays divided into acts. Previously, once started they would run on to the end. With increasingly elaborate scenery and effects, this gave breaks in the action for costume changes and any necessary re-dressing of the stage.**
- **A mid-play interval. Originally this may have been to allow staff to trim and relight candles which otherwise wouldn't last the length of the performance, but it quickly became an opportunity for fashionable playgoers to stroll about and see and be seen by their friends.**
- **Music as a regular, organised part of the performance. Some of the more spectacular aspects of masques, of the kind produced at court by Ben Jonson and Inigo Jones, were increasingly introduced as 'plays within a play'. Now largely obsolete, these formal, visually arresting bits of stagecraft remained popular throughout the Jacobean period and would last into the Restoration years.**

Below: A portrait of Inigo Jones, genius masque-stager, above a sketch of the Cockpit-in-Court, an early theatre near the Palace of Whitehall.

Left: Map showing the locations of the main London playhouses before 1642.

Blackfriars, (first) 1576–1584
Blackfriars, (second) 1596–1655
Curtain, 1577–after 1627
Fortune, (first) 1600–1621
Fortune, (second) 1623–1661
Globe, (first) 1599–1613
Globe, (second) 1614–1645
Hope, 1613–after 1682
Phoenix or Cockpit, 1617–after 1664
Red Bull, about 1605–after 1663
Rose, 1587–1605
Salisbury Court, 1629–1666
Swan, 1595–after 1632
Theatre, 1576–1598
Whitefriars, about 1605–1614

A Burst of Energy

The Romances
Shakespeare's romances, as the four late plays *Pericles*, *Cymbeline*, *The Winter's Tale* and *The Tempest*, are known, are romantic more in the sense of fairy tales than conventional love stories.

The romances were written between 1608 and 1611. Shakespeare had completed his trio of great tragedies – *Macbeth*, *Othello* and *King Lear*. *Coriolanus* and *Antony and Cleopatra* were in performance, too. By 1608, he was probably ready for a change, having turned out a production line of highly regarded plays ever since the company had come under the King's patronage. The King's Men were being summoned to perform at court more and more often, and the new plays offered enough plot twists and visual surprises to appeal to even the most jaded nobility. At this point in his career, Shakespeare had abandoned obedience to Aristotelian principles: these plays' timeframes and locations are, often literally, all over the place.

'Beware of trusting feigned beggars or fawning felons.'
Simon Forman, *The Book of Plaies*.
Forman, a doctor and astrologer, saw *The Winter's Tale* at the Globe in 1611, and his handwritten journal provides our only contemporary on-the-spot account. But his review concentrates largely on the no-good pedlar Autolycus. Sadly, he doesn't mention either the living statue or the bear.

Friend and Detractor

Not everyone admired the romances. In his 1613 play *Bartholomew Fair*, Ben Jonson, who was Shakespeare's friend (though sometimes a snarky one), has a character mock them, saying, 'He is loath to make nature afraid in his plays, like those that beget *Tales*, *Tempests*, and such like Drolleries…', implying that Jonson's is the voice of good, plain sense, away from the silly and the fantastic. We can't know how serious Jonson was, but he may not have approved of his fellow playwright's late adoption of masque-like interludes, magical 'happenings', such as the resurrection of Hermione at the end of *The Winter's Tale*, and increasingly exotic stage directions ('Exit, pursued by a bear' is from the same play). Real masques, after all, were very much Jonson's territory.

Opposite: The physician Simon Forman, whose contemporary notes on theatre visits were brief but pithy, alongside a 1904 illustration of the pedlar Autolycus from *The Winter's Tale*.

Below: Design for a 19th-century staging of *The Winter's Tale* alongside an illustration of Posthumus and Imogen, from *Cymbeline*, by Henry Justice Ford, from the turn of the 20th century.

The Tempest

A New Fantasy

***The Tempest* is the last play of which Shakespeare was sole author, and its themes of magic and renunciation make for a triumphant final hurrah. First performed as part of the winter season of 1611, it remains highly popular over four centuries later.**

Unusually for Shakespeare there's no traceable source for the central plot, the exile of the magician Prospero, Duke of Milan, and his daughter Miranda on a remote island, disrupted when a shipwreck washes up his usurper and a motley crew of other survivors. Scattered about the island, they encounter numerous enchantments before the play is resolved. The story was Shakespeare's own invention, but it reflects the influence of contemporary travellers' tales. The unnamed island is in the Mediterranean, but Shakespeare's imagination was primed by accounts from further afield – in particular, William Strachey's *True Repertory of the Wreck and Redemption of Sir Thomas Gates, Knight, upon the Islands of the Bermudas*, which was attracting a lot of attention in London. The colonial ambitions of the country King James had just christened 'Great Britain' were getting

Opposite left: Prospero, Miranda, Caliban and Ariel shown in a highly fantastical style, in an engraving made in about 1810 by the fashionable artist Henry Fuseli.

Opposite right: An 18th-century woodcut of a cannibal, similar to those used to illustrate the travel books to which Shakespeare would have had access.

Left: A watercolour of Act 1, Scene 2, in which Ferdinand, the shipwrecked prince, is puzzled by the music played by an invisible Ariel.

going, and citizens were agog to hear more of the discovery and conquest of distant lands. Add in Montaigne's 1580 essay, *Of Cannibals*, discussing the civilised habits of the regrettably cannibal inhabitants of Brazil – possibly an inspiration for the not-so-civilised Caliban? – and we have an enticing line-up of exotic ingredients.

This Rough Magic...

The Tempest's not-so-rough portrayals of magic, particularly characterised by the ethereal spirit Ariel, were no doubt helped in staging by professional musical accompaniment. And at the betrothal party of Miranda to Ferdinand, Shakespeare takes full advantage of equally novel staging effects when Prospero miraculously produces a full-on masque out of thin air, or, more likely, lowered from the roof.

'Now my charms are all o'erthrown And what strength I have's mine own Which is most faint...'

—*The Tempest*, Act 5, Epilogue

Stratford Business

SIBLINGS AND CHILDREN
Whether Shakespeare was in London or Stratford, the course of family life back in Warwickshire went on. Here's a brief recap.

Below: Southwark Cathedral, where Edmund Shakespeare was buried in 1607.

Opposite left: The frontispiece of the medical work written by Susanna Shakespeare's husband John Hall.

Opposite right: Wine merchants like Thomas Quiney, Judith Shakespeare's husband, trading at a port.

William outlived all three of his brothers (as a sidenote, he was also the only one to marry – it may be that their father's failing fortunes had made the younger brothers poor matrimonial prospects just at the ages when they'd otherwise have become eligible). The youngest, Edmund followed him to London and into acting, but died aged 27 in 1607. 'Edmund Shakespeare a player' had a pricey 20-shilling funeral – probably financed by William – and is buried in Southwark Cathedral.

Details of the other two are even scantier. Gilbert became a haberdasher, seems to have spent time in London, was either partner or surrogate in some of his older brother's property deals, and died in 1612. Richard died in 1613. Both are buried in Holy Trinity Church in Stratford. Joan, the only surviving sister, married William Hart, a hat-maker, had four children and died in Stratford at the great age of 77.

Susanna and Judith

Unlike their uncles, Shakespeare's two daughters both married. Susanna made a match with a doctor, John Hall, in 1607. He became a name in his own right, being one of the first to keep extensive case notes – *Select Observations on English Bodies of Eminent Persons in Desperate Diseases* – which would be published as a guide for later physicians in 1657.

Judith's choice was more vexed: she married Thomas Quiney, a wine and tobacco merchant, in February 1616, a few months before Shakespeare's death. They had a rushed wedding during Lent, without getting the special licence required, and Quiney became the subject of local scandal when, just after the marriage, he was named as the father of the child of a local girl who had died giving birth. This would have immediate consequences for the couple's inheritance from Judith's father.

> **'Fathers, from hence trust not your daughters' minds By what you see them act'**
>
> —*Othello*, Act 1, Scene 1

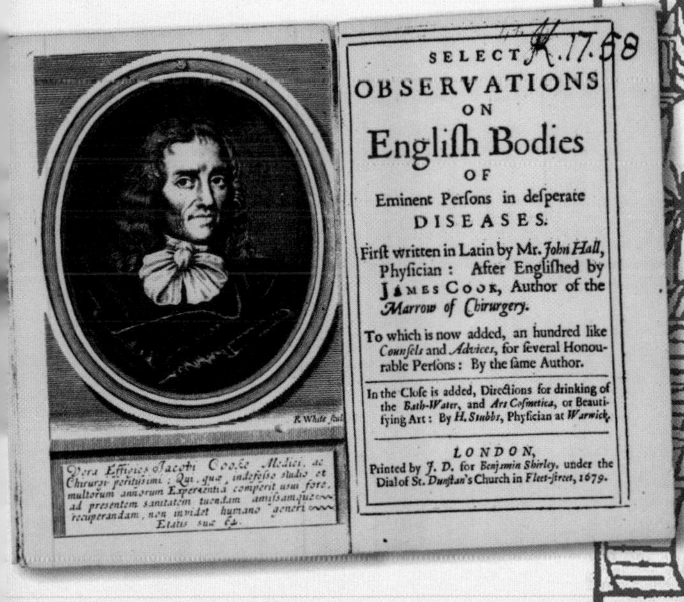

SELECT OBSERVATIONS ON English Bodies OF Eminent Persons in desperate DISEASES.

First written in Latin by Mr. *John Hall*, Physician: After Englished by JAMES COOK, Author of the *Marrow of Chirurgery*.

To which is now added, an hundred like *Counsels* and *Advices*, for several Honourable Persons: By the same Author.

In the Close is added, Directions for drinking of the *Bath-Water*, and *Ars Cosmetica*, or Beautifying Art: By *H. Stubbs*, Physician at *Warwick*.

LONDON, Printed by *J. D.* for *Benjamin Shirley*, under the Dial of St. *Dunstan's* Church in *Fleet-street*, 1679.

John Fletcher

Born to Write

In the early 1610s the name of John Fletcher begins to be associated with the King's Men. Shakespeare's junior by 15 years, he was already a celebrated and popular playwright, although his family background had made it an unusual choice of career.

Fletcher's father, Richard, was in the church, and would ultimately become Bishop of London – in an odd sidenote, as Queen Elizabeth's chaplain, he had officiated at the execution of Mary, Queen of Scots. John was born in Rye and was clearly precocious, attending Corpus Christi College in Cambridge (at the age of 11!) before starting a writing career. In the mid-1590s, after the death of his father, he's believed to have lived for a while with his uncle Giles, a poet and diplomat, in Bishopsgate Street in London. At the time, Shakespeare had lodgings in the same street, so it's probable that the two knew of each other long before they worked together.

Right: Unlike Shakespeare or Ben Jonson, Fletcher was a university man, who attended Corpus Christi College (below) in Cambridge.

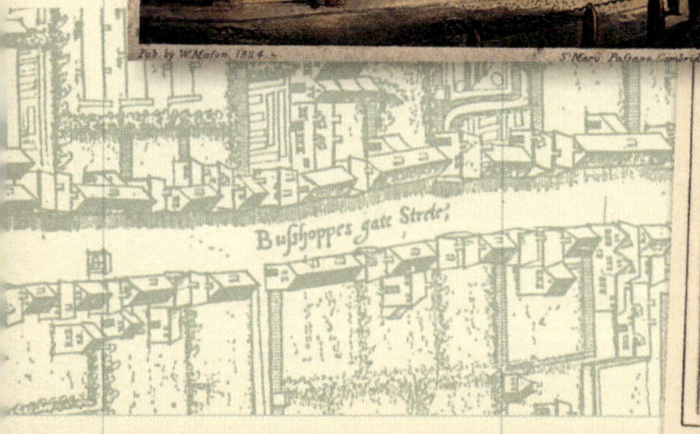

The Maides Tragedy.

AS IT HATH BEENE diuers times Acted at the *Blacke-friers* by the KINGS Maiesties Seruants.

LONDON

Printed for *Francis Constable* and are to be sold at the white Lyon ouer against the great North doore of *Pauls Church*. 1619.

Above: Francis Beaumont, Fletcher's first writing partner, with whom he collaborated on, among other plays, *The Maid's Tragedy*.

Beaumont and Fletcher

Fletcher had been employed working with the children's companies at the Blackfriars Theatre before 1608, regularly writing in collaboration with other makers. Today he's best known for his close partnership with Francis Beaumont – of their joint works, *Philaster* and *The Maid's Tragedy*, both from around 1609, proved particularly popular. *Philaster*, set in Sicily, and with a complex, bittersweet plot of mixed motives and mistaken identities, is the first Beaumont & Fletcher work known to have been performed by the King's Men, with stagings at the Globe, at Blackfriars and even, over the winter of 1612, at court. Like Shakespeare, Fletcher excelled at energetic, action-packed plays, and he was known for accomplished tragicomedies that could move an audience towards one reaction or other at will. In 1613 Beaumont married and seems subsequently to have withdrawn from writing plays, leaving Fletcher free to explore a closer collaboration with the King's Men.

'Ask how to live? Write, write, write, anything; The world's a fine believing world, write news.'

—*The Tragedy of Valentinian*, c.1610. Fletcher urges others to live by his own rules, in an early play performed by the King's Men

Working in Tandem

SHAKESPEARE AND FLETCHER Shakespeare's career had begun writing in partnership; now, in the 1610s, he was once again working in collaboration.

Theatre companies wanted to get their plays promptly into performance in the best fettle possible (one might draw an analogy with hit TV series or movies today); it was accepted that production was often a team effort. After Shakespeare started to withdraw from his involvement with the King's Men there may have been an agreement that John Fletcher, with a reputation then equal to his own, would replace him as house writer. Was it formal, or simply an understanding? Did Shakespeare want to retire? Was he ill? We'll never know. Whatever the reason, the final three plays were credited with joint authorship: Fletcher and Shakespeare.

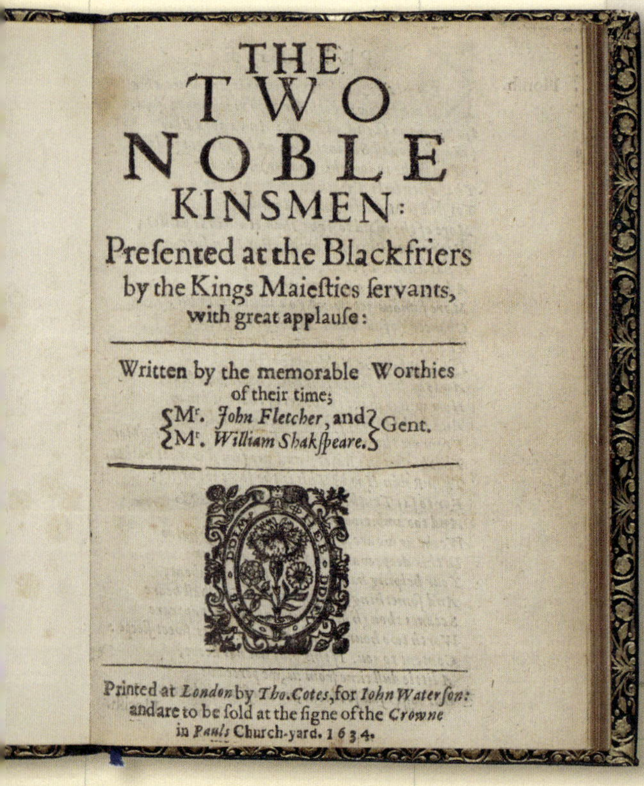
THE TWO NOBLE KINSMEN:
Presented at the Blackfriers by the Kings Maiesties servants, with great applause:
Written by the memorable Worthies of their time;
Mr. John Fletcher, and Mr. William Shakspeare. Gent.
Printed at London by Tho. Cotes, for Iohn Waterson: and are to be sold at the signe of the Crowne in Pauls Church-yard. 1634.

Who Wrote What?

The two that survive are neither playwright's best work; today they're treated more as oddities than masterpieces. *The Two Noble Kinsmen* and *Henry VIII* (first performed as *All is True*) were probably written in 1613. *The Two Noble Kinsmen* has roots in Chaucer – the story originates in *The Knight's Tale* – and has a complex plot with perpetual, almost frantic, action. *Henry VIII*, on the other hand, is a straight history play structured around the love story of the King and Anne Bullen (Boleyn), ending with the birth of Elizabeth and foretelling her future greatness. Both plays seem to have been written in sections by the playwrights, their not-very-similar styles sometimes causing a slight jarring of the gears.

CARDENIO: THE MISSING PLAY

The third collaboration is lost. *Cardenio* was performed for the court as part of the winter season of 1612, so was probably written slightly earlier than the other two. The plot derived from a story in Cervantes' *Don Quixote* – itself an indication of Fletcher's involvement; he was an enthusiastic user of Spanish sources, while Shakespeare was far more likely to turn to those from France or Italy. Because we don't have it, it's tempting to imagine that, of the three plays, it was the work of genius, but realistically it's most likely that it was workmanlike. Rediscovering it, though, remains a Shakespeare enthusiast's daydream.

Opposite: *The Two Noble Kinsmen* and *Henry VIII*, for which a 19th-century costume design is shown, right, were Shakespeare's final two works.

Above: Shakespeare and Fletcher's collaboration extended over at least three plays, one of which was the lost *Cardenio*.

The Globe Burns Down

The Beginning of the End
Fire was a well-recognised danger in London, with its packed-together, mostly wooden buildings. On 29 June 1613, during a performance of Shakespeare and Fletcher's new play *All is True* (*Henry VIII*), stage cannon were fired to mark Henry's entrance, with catastrophic results.

Sparks blew up to the thatch, which caught within minutes. At first the audience, absorbed by the play, didn't notice, but it was a hot summer's day and the flames spread quickly until the O-shaped roof was a circle of fire. Remarkably, given that the building was packed, there don't seem to have been any serious casualties, but the company had to watch as their theatre burned to the ground.

'...the fire catched... and there burned so furiously, as it consumed the whole house and all in less than two hours (the people having enough to do to save themselves)...'

—Letter from Thomas Lorkin to Sir Thomas Puckering, 30 June 1613, a day after the conflagration

Rebuilding

A handsome new Globe – this time with a tiled roof replacing the thatch – was built and opened by February 1614. It cost the King's Men £1,400 to rebuild. But Shakespeare's name doesn't appear on the list of contributors; a strong sign that by then he had begun to withdraw from the company.

Previously scholars have placed him back in Stratford more or less permanently from a year or two earlier, although he'd bought his first and only London property, a lodging in Blackfriars, in March 1611, which seems to indicate that he expected to be there at least some of the time. But there's no reason to suppose that he didn't continue to shuttle between London and Stratford quite often: plays were still being written and there was still London business to attend to. That he didn't help to finance the new theatre, though, is surely a clear indication that he considered his close involvement with the Globe, and by extension his London life, was over.

Opposite: Once alight, wood-and lathe-buildings like the Globe burned rapidly.

Below: The Globe was rebuilt within the year; here, a plan and panorama show its fine new incarnation.

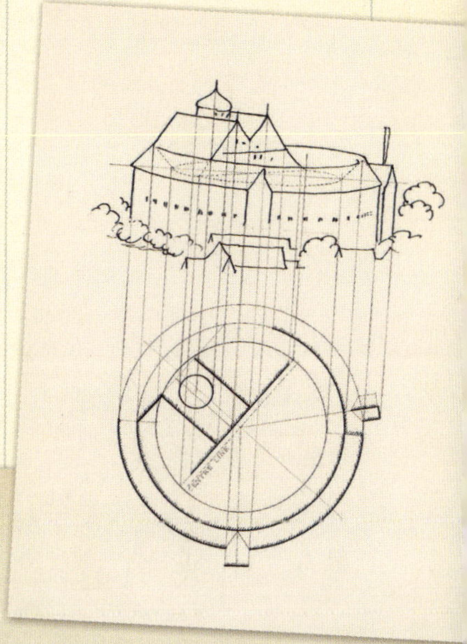

CHAPTER FIVE

DEATH AND AFTER

Death in Stratford

'A NECESSARY END'
William Shakespeare was interred at Holy Trinity Church on 25 April 1616. Burials usually took place within a day or two of death, so he died on or around 23 April, which would have been his 52nd birthday.

He seems to have been at New Place, in his own bed, having been attended by Susanna's doctor-husband John Hall. He must have known, or at least suspected, that he was very ill when he revised his will on 25 March. In the 16th century, wills were usually made when the subject felt they were close to death; although we don't know what Shakespeare died of, one suggestion has been typhoid fever. Spread through poor hygiene and incubated in dirty water, before the discovery of antibiotics, typhoid was often fatal. The ebb and flow of the disease arc takes about four weeks, so it's a reasonable guess. Fifty years after his death John Ward, the local vicar, noted down an old piece of local gossip – that 'Shakespeare, Drayton [the poet Michael Drayton, who was a local man] and Ben Jonson had a merry meeting, and it seems drank too hard for Shakespeare died of a fever there contracted', but although it's a good story it seems a rather unlikely one.

'We wondered, Shakespeare, that thou went'st so soon,
From the world's stage to the grave's tiring room.'

—James Mabbe, from the commemorative piece printed in the First Folio in 1623

How Old Was Old?

Some modern sources refer to Shakespeare as an old man 'for the period'; others say that, much like now, he'd have been perceived as being well into middle age. Plenty of people lived to old age in Tudor and Jacobean times – the biggest difference between then and now is that far more people of all ages died from diseases that would now be curable, so life expectancy was generally less predictable. Shakespeare wasn't very old for his times, nor would he then have been thought so.

Opposite left: Holy Trinity, where Shakespeare is buried alongside other members of his family.

Opposite right: New Place, where Shakespeare died in April 1616.

Below: A 19th-century illustration of an ageing Shakespeare, surrounded by books and manuscripts.

Shakespeare's Will

A Prudent Legacy
Everyone remembers Shakespeare's sole bequest to his wife was the 'second-best bed'. But his will has plenty of other interesting aspects, although it's not in itself an engaging read – it is, after all, a legal document, not a work of literature.

It is clearly based on earlier versions. All three pages are signed by Shakespeare, the third with a wavery signature, as if handling the quill was too much for him. The inventory to go with it hasn't survived, so we don't know, for example, if he left books and, if so, what they were.

The Man of Business

It's the will of a smart man of property. His daughters Susanna and Judith are treated very differently. Judith, freshly married to Thomas Quiney, gets a complicated financial deal, rewritten more or less to marginalise her husband. Quiney was probably an especial disappointment to Shakespeare as he was the son of Richard Quiney, a longtime friend of the family. (Margaret Wheeler, the woman Quiney junior had made pregnant, had died in childbirth a fortnight earlier, so the insult would have been fresh in Shakespeare's mind.) Susanna, however, is left the land he owned, plus New Place, the original family home in Henley Street, and the property in Blackfriars, with a line passing them down to her heirs. If she doesn't produce a male heir – and she didn't – it passes to her daughter, Elizabeth Hall.

There are a number of bequests. Seven men – four Stratford locals and three colleagues in the King's Men – Richard Burbage, John Heminges and Henry Condell – are left amounts to buy themselves memorial rings. His sister Joan gets £100 and all his clothes. And the second-best bed? It was probably the bed the couple slept in – the best bed being reserved for guests. Maybe Shakespeare depended on Susanna, who he clearly regarded as a safe pair of hands, to look after her mother. We simply can't know.

'…'tis our fast intent
To shake all cares and
business from our age;
Conferring them on
younger strengths…'

—*King Lear*, Act 1, Scene 1

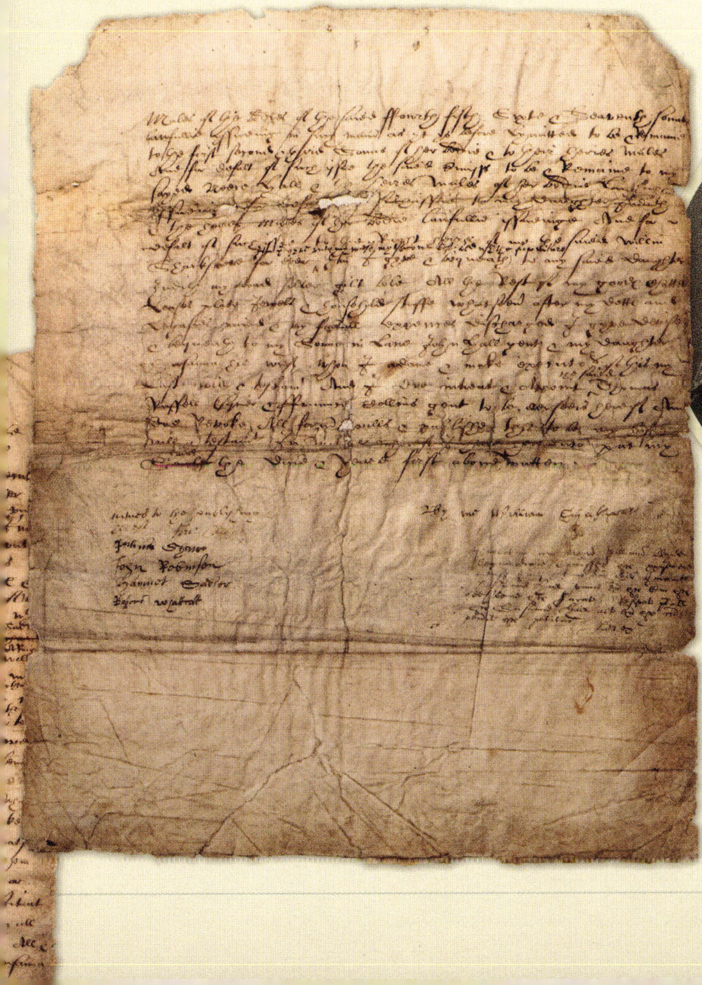

Above: A 19th-century engraving of Shakespeare.

Left: The three pages of Shakespeare's will, with all its amendments and updates, including the bequest for memorial rings for seven friends, including his colleague in the King's Company, Henry Condell.

Local Remembrance

Memorials
In time, Shakespeare would be appropriately remembered in the wider world. Stratford, though, where he was seen both as the local gentleman who had done well for himself and the literary talent who charmed London audiences, celebrated its eminent son in the local church.

If you visit Holy Trinity Church today, you'll find Shakespeare's monument in the chancel. In an elaborate, carved stone frame, topped by his coat of arms, itself flanked by cherubs and finished with a skull, the great man is shown as a seated bust. (Only the nobility got full-length memorials.) His left hand rests on a quire of paper laid on the cushion in front of him, while the right holds an appropriate quill. The inscription, in both Latin and English, celebrates his 'quick nature' and his 'living art'. The portrait, with its neat beard and strongly receding hairline, though fuller-faced than the engraving in the First Folio, matches our modern idea of how Shakespeare looked.

When did it go up? The monument was there by 1623, because it gets a mention in the First Folio; it also appears, not terribly recognisably, in William Dugdale's *Antiquities of*

Warwickshire of 1656 – your memorial only got an engraving if your descendants covered the £5 cost to the publisher; the surviving Shakespeares evidently felt the price was worth it. Shakespeare may have financed the monument before his death, or the efficient Susanna or other relatives or friends may have commissioned it. The stone bust has been repainted many times, and the quill and paper are probably later additions – the earliest drawings are shown without it.

Opposite: View through to the chancel of Holy Trinity Church, where Shakespeare's memorial is mounted high on the wall.

Below: Over time, Shakespeare's likeness, with the high forehead and neat beard, was enshrined in countless reproductions until it became instantly recognisable.

A Blunt Warning

Shakespeare's grave is also in the chancel. The slab lies alongside other family graves and expresses itself much more frankly than the monument – in words that may have been penned by the man himself. It seems unlikely that any future visitors will disobey.

'Good frend, for Jesus sake forbeare To digg the dust encloased heare, Bleste be ye man yt spares thes stones, And curst be ye yt moves my bones.'

—Shakespeare's memorial slab, complete with threat

The Family

What Happened Next
In the decades that followed Shakespeare's death, the family story doesn't supply anything very remarkable – it was as though, having produced a genius, the Shakespeares once more retreated into comparative obscurity.

Anne Shakespeare died in 1623 and was buried beside her husband. John and Susanna Hall continued to live in Hall's Croft, a handsome house they had built in Stratford in 1613. Dr Hall died in 1635, Susanna followed him in 1649. Both are buried near her father in Holy Trinity Church.

Despite its inauspicious start, Thomas and Judith Quiney's marriage was long-lasting and produced three sons. Tragically, though, all died young: the first, named Shakespeare for Judith's father, as a baby, then both Richard and Thomas as young men, in 1639, probably from plague.

'Witty above her sex, but that's not all,
Wise to salvation was good Mistris Hall.'

—Susanna Shakespeare's epitaph: flattering, but lacking the vigour of her father's

This left Elizabeth Hall as Shakespeare's only surviving grandchild. She was given the all-round education of a gentlewoman, and her first marriage, in 1626, was to Thomas Nash, a barrister and the son of an old family friend. He died in 1647; in 1649 Elizabeth remarried, this time to John Bernard, an MP and landowner with an estate in Northamptonshire. He was knighted in 1661 by Charles II (the couple were fervent royalists), and she became Lady Elizabeth Bernard, completing her social climb. Neither marriage produced children, and Elizabeth died in 1670, bringing William Shakespeare's direct line to an end.

A Near Miss

In 1662, Stratford got a new vicar. John Ward was a Shakespeare enthusiast, and there are several entries about the playwright in his notebooks (one of these is the mention of the 'merry meeting' that caused the fever that killed Shakespeare). There's also an intriguing note about his intention to visit 'Mrs Queeny', but Judith Quiney died the year he was appointed. It seems the visit never happened – a lost chance for personal memories of Shakespeare that leaves us with one of the great 'what-ifs?' of literary history.

Opposite: Hall's Croft, where John Hall and Susanna Shakespeare lived after 1613, and Holy Trinity, where she and her husband are buried alongside her father.

Left: Elizabeth Hall, Susanna's daughter and Shakespeare's last direct descendant, painted with her first husband John Nash.

Back with the King's Men

BUSINESS AS USUAL
Back in London Shakespeare would have been missed; after all, he had had a close association with many of his colleagues for over 20 years, going back to the early days of the Lord Chamberlain's Men. The life of the company, however – rehearsals, tours, court performances – went on.

The playwright's life had always been divided between Stratford and London, and in the last year or two his output had (finally) reduced. But his plays were performed just as frequently in the years immediately after his death: Richard Burbage, the public face of Shakespeare's words, had become famous in his friend's great leading roles and went on playing them until his own death.

End of an Age

The company continued to change. Robert Armin, the rueful clown, had died in 1615, to be replaced by John Shank as lead comedian, and there was a slow turnover of other personnel as actors' lives changed, apprentices were promoted and fresh talent was found.

'Burbage, the player, has vouchsafed to die!
Therefore, in London is not one eye dry:
The deaths of men who act our Queens and Kings,
Are now more mourn'd than are the real things'

—From an anonymous poem satirising public grief on the death of Burbage – Queen Anne died just a week before the actor, her passing marked by much less fuss

The final blow to the original company came with the death of Richard Burbage on 9 March 1619, which was greeted with a huge outpouring of affection and grief in the capital. At the time of Burbage's death King James had just issued a renewed royal patent, naming the company's joint shareholders, so its patronage was safe. Cuthbert Burbage seems to have taken a backseat after his brother died, although he continued as a keeper until his own death in 1636. Overall, though, the King's Men must have been competently managed, as they remained productive and successful until all theatres and companies were closed by Parliament at the outbreak of the Civil War in 1642.

Opposite: Richard Burbage died in 1619, just three years after his colleague.

Below: Charles I, left, and Sir Edward Walker, his Secretary at War, shown after the outbreak of the English Civil War in 1642.

Collected Works

Making History
We have heard of Shakespeare because his plays are in print. But in the early 17th century this was far from a given. At the time of his death, his plays were scattered far and wide and only 18 had been published.

Familiar faces to their audiences, actors were the stars of the theatre. In Elizabeth's reign the name of a playwright, however popular the play, might not be known; by the first quarter of the 17th century, that was slowly changing. Plays that made it as far as publication increasingly featured the author's name on the title page.

An Innovation

Ben Jonson, never one to hide his light under a bushel, was the first to produce a collection of his theatrical writings. Already highly thought of at court, he was appointed Poet Laureate, an altogether new role, by the King in 1616. In the same year, *The Workes of Benjamin Jonson* were published in a handsome folio format, containing the nine of his plays that already existed in print, a number of masques and 'entertainments' – the latter the rather odd-seeming mix of poetry, oration and acting that were put together for special occasions at court – and a good deal of poetry.

Jonson had begun collecting and editing his writings in 1612. While the publication of long-form poetry and collections of shorter poems were familiar and admired (*Venus and Adonis* remained Shakespeare's best-selling work for some time after his death and had something of a cult following among romantic Oxford students), putting a play into print for literary rather than strictly practical – that is, for staging – purposes was a new idea. The publication of Jonson's collected work was important: it lifted the 'maker's' role from the ephemeral to something much more significant and permanent.

Opposite: Ben Jonson's *Collected Works*, published in 1616, in folio form, set a grand precedent which Shakespeare's First Folio would follow when it was published seven years later.

Below: An enduring sleeper hit, *Venus and Adonis* kept on selling even decades after its author's death.

'Pray tell me Ben, where doth the mystery lurk,
What others call a play you call a work?'

—Lines questioning Jonson's presumption in elevating his plays to published 'works'. From *Witts Recreations*, a 1640 miscellany of humorous pieces.

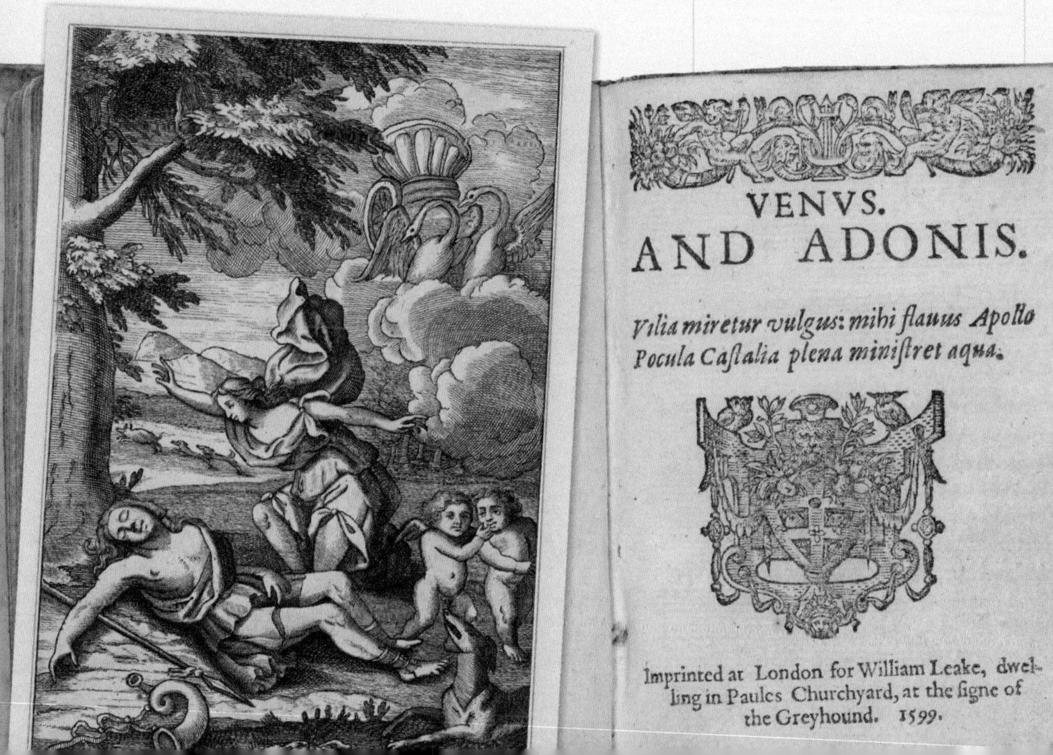

The First Folio

Planning Ahead

Shakespeare would have known about Jonson's collected works, and it's possible that before his death he had begun to plan something similar for himself. Two of his colleagues in the King's Men, John Heminges and Henry Condell, would see the First Folio through.

Both Heminges and Condell were longstanding members of the company and, along with Burbage, had been left money for memorial rings in Shakespeare's will. (Could this have been a reminder that a promise about a literary legacy had been made?)

Lining up 36 plays for a single publication was a huge task. Twenty-two, including the 18 already published, had been licensed and were listed in the Stationers' Register; the others had only ever existed in script form, and needed tracking down and cleaning up. Luckily Heminges and Condell proved to be perfect for the job, which called for stamina, determination and business savvy.

Getting into Print

By the end of 1622 the project was nearly finished. That autumn it appears in the Stationers' Register listings of forthcoming books, used to advertise to the Frankfurt Book Fair, then as now one of the largest international booksellers' gatherings:

'Playes, written by M. William Shakespeare, all in one volume, printed by Isaack Isaggard [Jaggard], in fol.' The print run of around 750 copies, priced at 15 shillings unbound, or 20 shillings in a plain calf binding, was registered for publication in November 1623.

Below: In the printshop. Even after all the plays had been tracked down, the typesetting and printing of such a huge project was extraordinarily time-consuming.

Opposite: A copy of the finished book, this one in a fine leather binding. Around 750 were printed, of which 235 copies survive.

The Stationers' Register

This list was the method by which the Stationers' Company, a trade guild, managed the rights for booksellers to print and sell authors' works. Once a bookseller had agreed with an author to publish a work, he paid to get his right listed in the Register. Officially this should have made it easy to keep track of who owned rights; unofficially, especially when they had been passed on as part of an inheritance, tracking them down could be a frustrating hunt.

'He was not for an age, but for all time!'

—Ben Jonson in full effusion mode, in the second of two laudatory poems he wrote for the First Folio

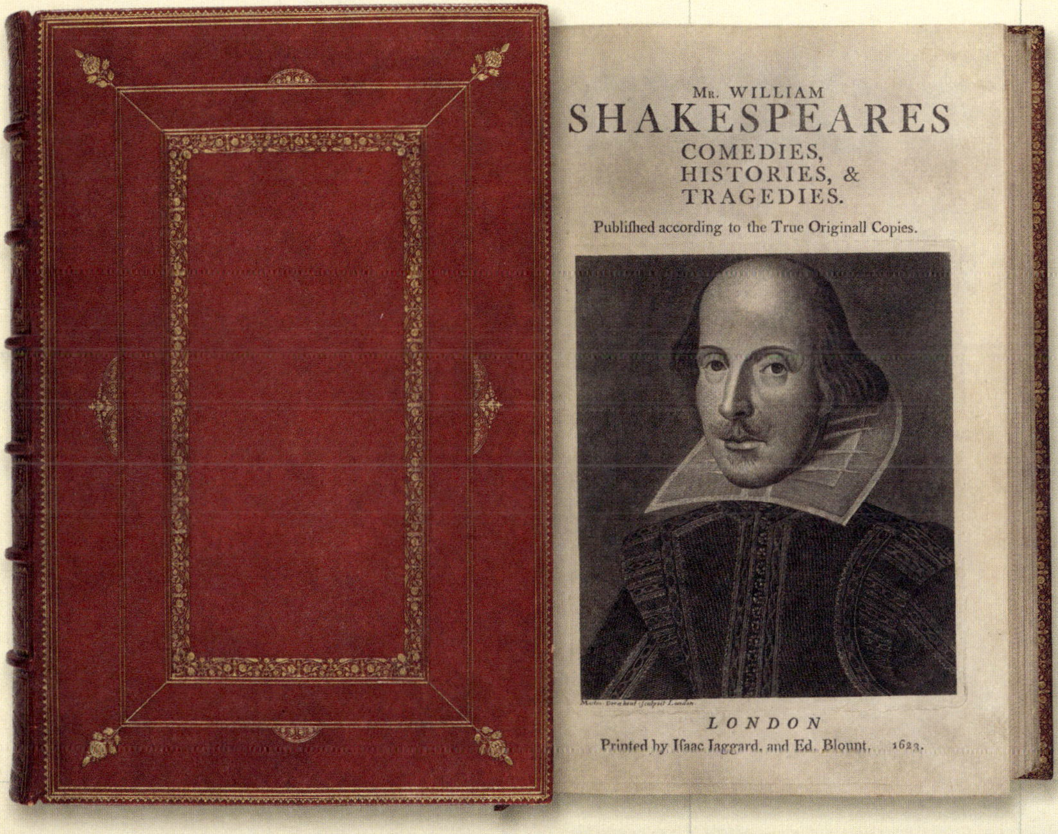

A Publishing Legacy

SHAKESPEARE FOR POSTERITY

Not only did it save the plays that might have been lost, but the First Folio also set firm some of the ways in which we still see Shakespeare and his works, from the familiar frontispiece portrait to its division of his plays into Comedies, Histories and Tragedies – how they have been categorised ever since.

Two plays that weren't included but that have been, at least partially, attributed – *Pericles, Prince of Tyre* and *The Two Noble Kinsmen* – took a long time to make it back into the canon, unlike, say, *Henry VIII*, although all are collaborative efforts. *Troilus and Cressida* made it into the Folio just under the wire – it isn't listed on the contents page because the rights were only cleared at the very last moment.

> 'His mind and hand went together: And what he thought, he uttered with that easiness, that we have scarce received from him a blot in his papers... Reade him therefore; and againe, and againe...'

—From Heminges and Condell's preface to the First Folio, with an approving comment on the cleanness of Shakespeare's copies. It marks the moment at which he is passed on to future readers.

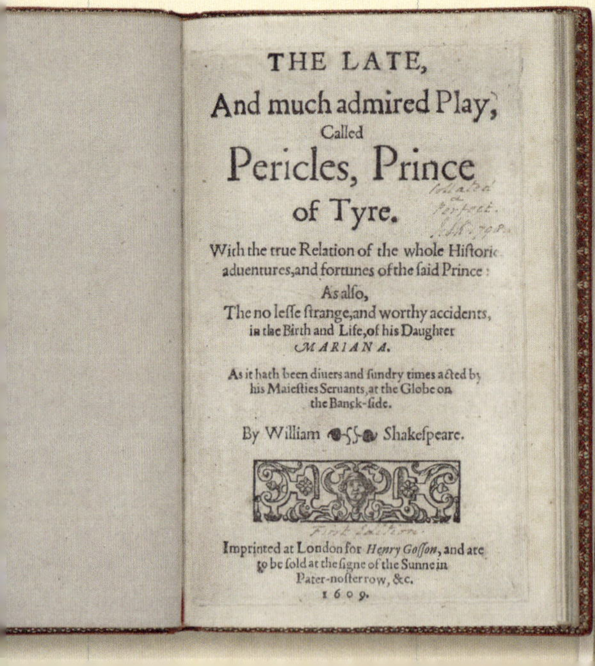
THE LATE,
And much admired Play,
Called
Pericles, Prince
of Tyre.
With the true Relation of the whole Historie, aduentures, and fortunes of the said Prince:
As alſo,
The no leſſe ſtrange, and worthy accidents, in the Birth and Life, of his Daughter
MARIANA.
As it hath been diuers and ſundry times acted by his Maieſties Seruants, at the Globe on the Banck-ſide.
By William Shakeſpeare.
Imprinted at London for Henry Goſſon, and are to be ſold at the ſigne of the Sunne in Pater-noſter-row, &c.
1609.

A Familiar Portrait

Apart from the monument in Stratford, the frontispiece is the only likeness we have of Shakespeare that we know was seen by those who knew him; Ben Jonson claimed it looked like his friend. It was by Martin Droeshout, a well-regarded engraver, although he was only 22 when it was made. There must have been some source material – a painting, a sketch? It may have been the more appealing but unconfirmed Chandos portrait, with its characterful face and gold earring, originally owned by William Davenant, one of Shakespeare's godsons and now in London's National Portrait Gallery. We don't know. The end result is clumsy – the face is lifeless, the receding hairline drawing our attention over any personality. Like it or loathe it, today it's the mental image that comes up when we hear Shakespeare's name.

Opposite: Frontispiece from a 1609 printing of *Pericles*, alongside an illustration of Marina being abducted by pirates.

Below left: Troilus, Cressida and Pandarus, from the play that only just made it into the First Folio.

Below right: The Chandos portrait, which gives a much more appealing idea of Shakespeare's appearance than Droeshout's rather lacklustre engraving.

End of an Era

The Civil War and After
English theatre as it had been known by Shakespeare and his contemporaries came to an end on 2 September 1642, when Parliament closed all the theatres and public entertainments were banned. There would be no more performances for nearly 20 years.

Puritans had long been outraged by the immorality of the theatre, and the opportunities it offered for airing contentious views – including political ones. When the war finally came to an end, Parliament victorious, in 1651, the shutdown continued under the Protectorate of Oliver Cromwell. By 1660, when Charles II became king, things had irrevocably changed.

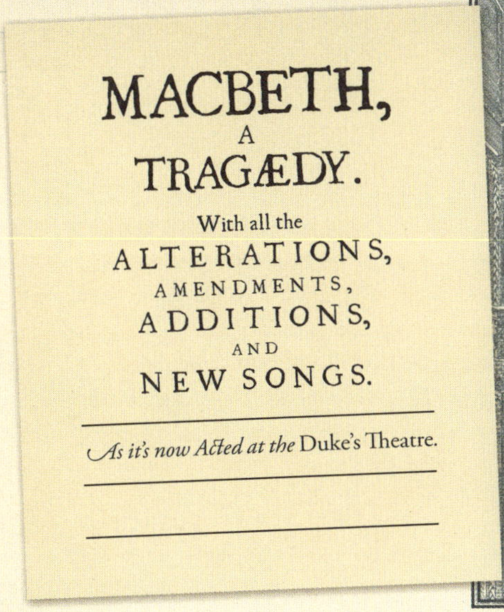
MACBETH,
A
TRAGÆDY.
With all the
ALTERATIONS,
AMENDMENTS,
ADDITIONS,
AND
NEW SONGS.

As it's now Acted at the Duke's Theatre.

All Change

Charles licensed the re-formed King's Men, now led by Thomas Killigrew. But there was a problem: not much theatrical tradition had survived the long break. A handful of the original players of the King's Men returned – originally apprentices or boy players who could now graduate to full acting parts. In the short-term, too, there were no new plays. Until London theatre recovered, there was a return to the greats of Jonson, Fletcher – and Shakespeare.

The second company licensed by the King was the Duke's Men, under the patronage of his brother, James, Duke of York. Of the two, they were the more innovative performers. What they didn't care for, they changed. Most performances now took place inside, with a number of new London theatres opening in the 1660s and '70s, led by the Vere Street Theatre, home to the King's Company, which opened in 1660. These took full advantage of the opportunities offered for lavish scenery and effects. New playwrights, including Nahum Tate (memorable for his happy-ending version of *King Lear*), John Dryden and William Davenant (who also led the Duke's Men and became a notable theatre manager) freely adapted old favourites. They were picking out material magpie-like, just as Shakespeare and Jonson had done 50 years earlier.

Opposite: Oliver Cromwell, the Lord Protector, under whom all performances were banned (left), and (right) Thomas Killigrew, the new manager of the post-war King's Men.

Above, from top left: Title page from the Restoration all-singing, all-dancing version of *Macbeth*; an interior view of the new Duke's Theatre; and a miniature of Charles II painted in around 1672.

Girls on Stage

New Age, New Rules
Restoration theatre brought another huge change: the licences given to the King's and Duke's Men in 1660 stated that all female roles could now be played by women. The wording goes further, decrying the previous boys-as-girls parts as 'scandalous and offensive'.

Social mores had shifted; it was now more immoral for a man to play a woman than for a woman to appear on a public stage. Where earlier playwrights had written plots incorporating women disguised as men partly as a way of making things easier for male actors, now the numerous woman-in-disguise parts allowed an actress to appear in a 'breeches' role, with the freedom to show her legs as well as her acting. The less cerebral members of the audience (diarist Samuel Pepys unsurprisingly among them) certainly approved.

Late Adopters

Women had acted on stage in Spain, France and Italy since the end of the 16th century. Charles II had spent much of his exile in Europe and would have seen actresses for himself. London was coming late to the party, but the companies quickly made up for it. In some cases, those rewriting older plays might seem, to us, to have gone overboard: *The Tempest,* revised in 1667 by Davenant and the newly fashionable poet and playwright John Dryden, introduced a sister for Caliban, a fellow female spirit for Ariel, and a second daughter for Prospero. Not only that, but Dryden's prologue patronises his predecessor, claiming that he has breathed new life into 'old Shakespear's honour'd dust'.

Seven years later the new version was converted into an opera, which became the most frequently staged *Tempest* until Victorian times. Shakespeare was still admired, but his originals had become resolutely unfashionable.

Opposite left: Margaret Hughes, who was the first woman to play Desdemona on the English stage in December 1660.

Opposite right: A 1926 illustration by Kitty Shannon, showing Nell Gwyn, mistress of Charles II, playing a breeches role in Dryden's play *Almanzor and Almahide*, in 1670.

Below: The celebrated German soprano Henriette Sontag who, in 1850, sang the role of Miranda in the operatic version of *The Tempest* to great acclaim.

'I saw women acte, a thing that I never saw before... and they performed it with as good a grace, action, gesture, and whatsoever convenient for a Player, as ever I saw any masculine Actor.'

—The traveller Thomas Coryat in Venice, on his first sight of actresses on stage, *Coryat's Crudities*, 1611

Did Shakespeare Write Shakespeare?

THE AUTHORSHIP QUESTION Some have found it difficult to reconcile a stolid Stratford businessman with the greatest playwright of his era. From the late 18th century some scholars argued that Shakespeare of Stratford hadn't written Shakespeare's works at all.

There were – and still are – enough believers in the idea for there to be a name for them: Anti-Stratfordians. They have included plenty of eminent people, such as Sigmund Freud and Mark Twain. The arguments against Stratford Shakespeare have included his relatively basic education – not advanced enough for him to have produced such work, it's felt – and too few provable links between the Stratford and London Shakespeares – though this isn't unusual when records were inevitably patchy. Perhaps there's also a longing for a more glamorous figure as a focus for all the bardolatry. Couldn't Jonson's 'Sweet Swan of Avon' be a bit more, well, sophisticated?

'...To be, or not to be, that is the question.'

—*Hamlet*, Act III, Scene 1

Alternative Shakespeares

If Shakespeare didn't author 38-plus plays and a good deal of poetry, who did? Of dozens of possible candidates, there are three clear favourites.

- **Front runner is Edward de Vere, Earl of Oxford, intellectual at the court of Elizabeth and accomplished writer. Why couldn't he just admit he wrote all these masterpieces? Too difficult to match with his high social standing, goes the argument of his advocates, the Oxfordians. He died in 1604, though, so would have had to have trusted allies to trickle out later plays posthumously.**

- **Second is Christopher Marlowe. He could certainly write, but his murder in 1593 would have made it difficult for him to have delivered all the way up to 1612. Followers of Marlowe-Shakespeare (Marlovians) claim he faked his own death and carried on writing under a different name.**

- **Sir Francis Bacon, the great Elizabethan philosopher and statesman comes in third. Baconians claim that he used his plays to put his political and philosophical beliefs into an artistic form. But it's hard to see how he would have made the time.**

That's just the leading three. In the end, unless you're a fervent Anti-Stratfordian, it might be simpler to believe that Shakespeare wrote Shakespeare.

Opposite: Sigmund Freud (left) and Mark Twain, leading members of the Anti-Stratfordian movement.

Below: Sir Francis Bacon, lawyer, scientist, philosopher and statesman, who also served as Solicitor General, Attorney General and Lord Chancellor. It's hard to believe that he could also have authored 38 plays.

The First Biography

THE MAN AND HIS WORK
For those who accept that Stratford Shakespeare and playwright Shakespeare are one and the same, there are still plenty of unanswered questions. Unfortunately, the 'first biography' of the Bard didn't do much to confirm the events of his life.

In 1709, Nicholas Rowe, a playwright and theatrical entrepreneur, contributed an extended introduction to a new six-volume edition of Shakespeare's plays. Amidst discussion of his works, *Some Account of the Life &c. of Mr William Shakespear* [sic] contains a number of anecdotes that had been collected from people who could, at a pinch, have met Shakespeare, but who were more likely merely to have known of him.

Teasing Out Information

Thomas Betterton was an actor with Davenant's Duke's Men in the 1680s. Today he's better known for having been commissioned by Rowe to go to Stratford and find what stories he could of the town's increasingly famous son.

Rowe was responsible for the first mention of various stories, including the one that had Shakespeare fleeing to London from a poaching charge; he also cites the link with the printer Richard Field, one of Shakespeare's few provable connections between Stratford and London.

Less convincingly, Rowe features some sentimental anecdotes, notably one about jolly old John Shakespeare, 'who spoke well tho' boldly of his Celebrated son. My Will, he said, is an Honest fellow, with a place at Court, but never too Lofty to crack a Jest with his old Dad'. Heartwarming but, given that John Shakespeare had now been dead for over a century, not altogether convincing. And when it comes to the playwright's London life, he includes some wholly unbelievable content featuring a positively flirty relationship between William Shakespeare and the Virgin Queen herself.

Left: A Victorian illustration of Shakespeare performing to an entranced Queen Elizabeth – the sort of unlikely friendship between the two that Rowe described.

Below: Nicholas Rowe was a successful playwright and poet. His 'life' of Shakespeare was written to introduce the Fourth Folio, a new edition of the collected plays.

Above: Thomas Betterton on stage as Hamlet, a role he played well into his '70s.

'The latter Part of his Life was spent, as all Men of good Sense will wish theirs may be, in Ease, Retirement, and Conversation of his Friends...'

—From *Some Account of the Life*, Rowe's sunny picture of Shakespeare's last years, 1709

Shakespeare in Translation

Early Days

Even if audiences didn't know who wrote them, it's likely that some of Shakespeare's plays were seen abroad within his lifetime. From the 1590s onwards, troupes of English players toured in Europe, where they were both popular and well-paid.

The English companies went down particularly well in Germany, the Netherlands and Denmark; the Landgrave of Hesse-Kassel even built a handsome theatre, the Ottoneum, for 'his' English players in 1605 (still standing in Kassel, although today it's a museum).

Conquering Europe

Over the 18th and early 19th centuries, Shakespeare started to be singled out to be read as well as performed. New translations were made by distinguished literary figures in Europe. Germany was the most enthusiastic adopter; by 1766, 22 plays were available in German. Young stars of the *Sturm und Drang* (Storm and Stress) movement, including Goethe and Schiller, took him as one of their own. The critic and translator August Schlegel, who by 1807 had made highly regarded translations of 13 of the plays, would declare Shakespeare to be '*ganz unser*' ('completely ours').

'Once I had read an entire play, I stood there like a blind man given the gift of sight by some miraculous healing touch.'

—Johann Wolfgang von Goethe enthusing, aged just 22, in 1771

France took to Shakespeare early, too, but was more ambivalent. The philosopher Voltaire was translating key speeches from the plays by the 1730s, but French theatre was based on order and classicism, and many felt Shakespeare was a disruptor. Like other revolutionaries, he broke through: the complete works were first translated into French by Pierre-Antoine de la Place in the late 1740s, and by 1769 *Hamlet* was on stage in Paris.

Shakespeare filtered through to southern Europe gradually, becoming more familiar in Italy and Spain in the early 19th century. Gradually his work was spreading ever further afield. He served as a model as well as a master: in 1825, the great Russian poet Alexander Pushkin claimed he had written his historical drama *Boris Godunov*, the story of a classic power struggle between warring rulers, 'according to the system of our father Shakespeare'.

Opposite: Schiller, left, and Goethe, both fervent admirers of Shakespeare.

Above: Voltaire, who had mixed feelings about Shakespeare, admitting his genius, but also describing his work as barbaric and uncontrolled.

Below: Title pages from a 1776 printing of the De la Place translations.

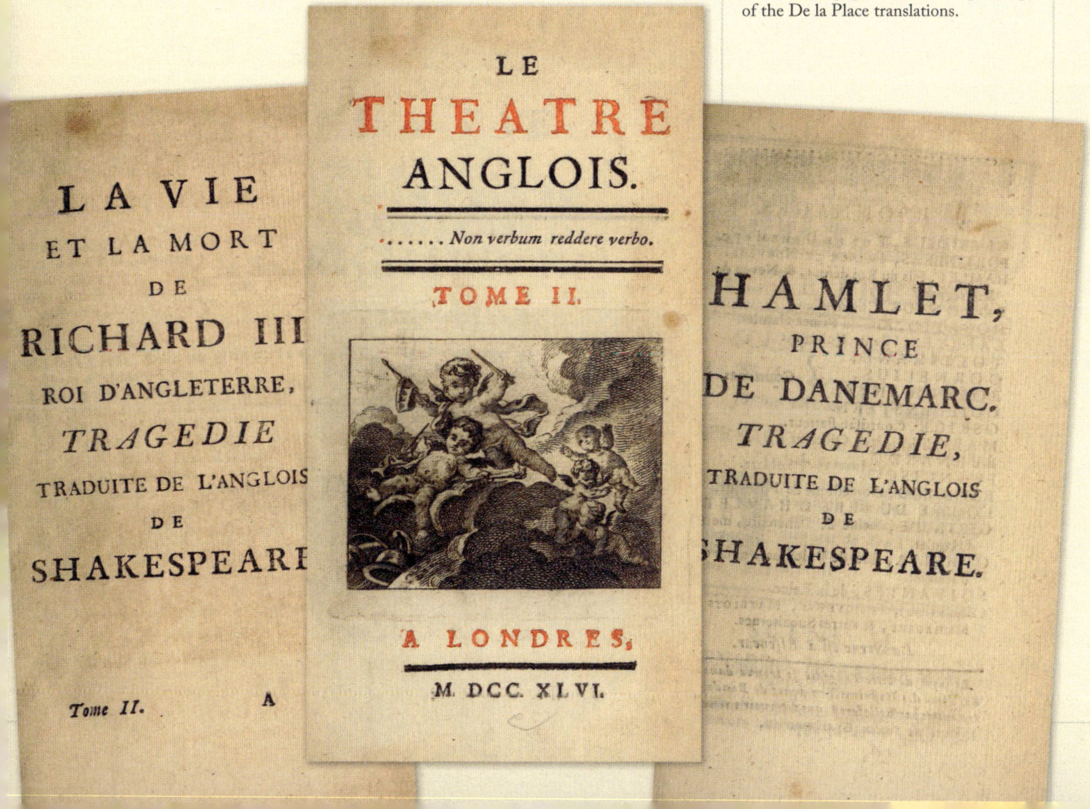

Everyman's Playwright

Garrick and After
The point at which Shakespeare becomes 'Shakespeare' – not just a highly regarded writer but the central figure of English literature – is often pinned to September 1769, when David Garrick, superstar of the London stage, held a Shakespeare Jubilee in Stratford.

He'd been invited by the town's corporation, and the event itself was not a great success – it was disrupted by appalling weather and floods. Some attendees felt that the activities, which included racing and a masked ball, were a vulgar grab on Shakespeare's name – for a Shakespeare event, it was all quite low on Shakespeare. But it marked the beginning of Stratford's tourist industry and elevated him to the status of people's playwright: universally familiar, even to people who weren't themselves playgoers.

'We did not get home till past six in the morning. I got about three hours' sleep... After the joy of the Jubilee came the uneasy reflection that I was in a little village in wet weather and knew not how to get away.'

—The diarist James Boswell suffering festival-goer's remorse after the Garrick Jubilee, in a letter to the *London Magazine*, September 1769

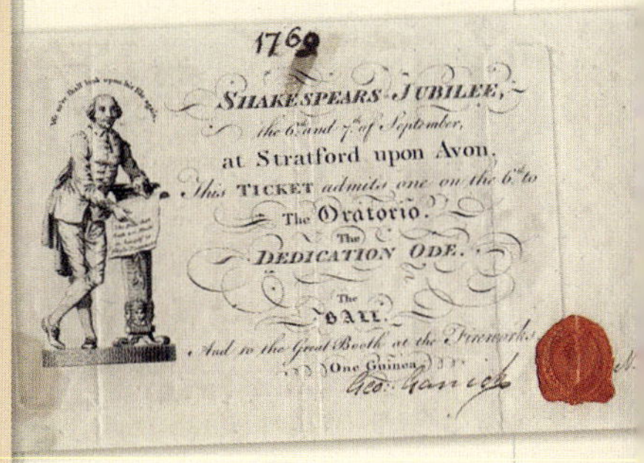

Opposite: Stratford cheerfully dressed up for the Jubilee in a 19th-century painting by Charles Knight.

Above left: A high point and one of the more faithfully Shakespearean parts of the Jubilee – David Garrick declaiming at the foot of the Bard's statue.

Above right: A Jubilee ticket admitting the holder to the oratorio, the dedication ode and the ball, at the price of a guinea.

Becoming Modern

Once the ball was rolling, nothing could stop it. Shakespeare's star rose even higher with the Victorians, who gave him the status of a (secular) god – sermons were based on carefully chosen quotations from his plays, while Henrietta Bowdler produced a heavily edited *Family Shakespeare*, safe for children (and unwittingly created the verb 'to bowdlerise', the process of removing lurking indelicacies).

Through the 20th century his work came under different kinds of scrutiny. At the scholarly end, university departments were studying the plays from literary and contextual viewpoints; in the popular culture arena, more films and TV programmes drew on the plays than those of any other author; even in psychoanalytic circles, Hamlet, Ophelia, Othello and Lear et al were all used to illustrate universal human dilemmas.

Media Shifts

'Shakespeare has never been a dead author. At every epoch, in every culture, he is alive, like an ocean in which every drop is on the move.'

—Veteran director Peter Brook, 2009

When Shakespeare's works were first shown on screen, directors didn't immediately take advantage of the new medium – star actors were simply turning in stage performances to a larger audience and with better props. A century on, there's much greater awareness of the possibilities, both on screen, and, revisited, on stage.

War and Peace

During the Second World War, Shakespeare was useful for propaganda on both sides. In 1944 *Henry V*, starring Laurence Olivier, England's leading man, offered up a glorified image of war to shore up flagging spirits; while the Reich Theatre Chamber, soberingly, made substantial changes to stage versions of *The Merchant of Venice*, to remove the subtleties Shakespeare worked into Shylock, and give the play a much more crudely anti-Semitic slant.

Into peacetime, cinema helped Shakespeare's global spread. *Macbeth*, *Hamlet* and *Romeo and Juliet* are probably the most frequently and variously adapted. Feudal Japan proved a magnetic setting for *Throne of Blood*, Akira Kurosawa's 1957 adaptation of *Macbeth*, while *Romeo and Juliet* is a prime example of a work that has flexed as needed. Shifting the setting from Verona to New York, *West Side Story* borrowed the plot and transformed it into a musical, becoming first a stage hit in 1957, then an instant classic on screen in 1961. In 1968 Franco Zeffirelli realised that a traditional play-as-film with actual teenagers in the lead roles could still touch a contemporary chord; by 1996 the star cross'd lovers had moved to a fictional city on America's west coast with Baz Luhrmann's glittering version, accessorised with cars and drugs.

West Side Story was an early move to borrow the plot but not the language – by 1999 *10 Things I Hate About You* had shifted *The Taming of the Shrew* to the dating scene of a US high school, while *The Lion King*, in both its screen and stage versions, (very) loosely adapts *Hamlet*. 'Straight' art-house retellings, such as the 2021 *The Tragedy of Macbeth*, directed by Joel Coen, remain popular, too.

Opposite left: Laurence Olivier woos Renée Asherson, playing Katherine, the French princess, in the fervently patriotic 1944 film of *Henry V*.

Opposite right: The 1961 poster for *West Side Story*, Bernstein and Sondheim's musical classic.

Below: Claire Danes and Leonardo di Caprio in Baz Luhrmann's *Romeo and Juliet* in 1996, convincing audiences as passionate teenagers.

'For all time'

Prophecy or Millstone? Jonson's effusion – 'He was not for an age, but for all time!' – which might have seemed excessive in 1623, is starting to look prophetic. Will Shakespeare outlast us all? The signs, four centuries on, are that he should be good for a few more.

He's already here, embedded in the culture and the language. Anthologies may be fond of pointing out that Shakespeare has been translated into more than 100 languages 'including Klingon', as though that were the ultimate badge of popularity, but it's probably this unconscious absorption into the language that marks him out as unique.

Everyone quotes Shakespeare without even being aware of it; hundreds of expressions – apple of your eye, laughing-stock, heart of gold, break the ice, and dozens of others – all originate with him and are still in constant use. And his popularity on stage, on screen and in study remains steady.

The Robben Island 'Bible'

On Robben Island, the jail in which South Africa's leading freedom fighters were incarcerated from the 1960s to the '90s, the contraband so-called 'Bible', smuggled in and circulated, was a collected Shakespeare. Used for solace and encouragement, the passages the prisoners found particularly inspiring are signed. In 1977, Nelson Mandela wrote his name beside this quote from *Julius Caesar*:
'It seems to me most strange that men should fear,
Seeing that death, a necessary end,
Will come when it will come.'

Ageing Well

In the 21st century there are new challenges. Shakespeare was a man of his time, too, and his writing is rooted in all sorts of beliefs which become difficult and unacceptable according to the era: earlier times got squeamish about the plays' sex and violence; now we can see them as racist, sexist and deeply colonialist, too. We can't dismiss the problems so what's the answer? As always, it's adaptation – we might no longer add characters to a line-up, but we're happy to switch gendered parts around, and to admit and work around values that we don't find acceptable. Shakespeare's work is so far strong enough to take anything thrown at it.

Opposite left: The familiar likeness that, today, is instantly recognisable as William Shakespeare.

Opposite right: The balcony scene from *Romeo and Juliet*, still a marker for instant romance after more than four centuries.

Below: A 19th-century panorama of characters from Shakespeare. Look closely and you should be able to find Falstaff, Rosalind and Celia, Lear and Cordelia, Olivia and Malvolio, Othello and Desdemona – and possibly one or two others.

References

Online

There's no shortage of excellent online sources, podcasts and everything else on Shakespeare. Three good starting points are:

The Folger Shakespeare Library
folger.edu
Based on the world's largest Shakespeare collection, in Washington, DC, the Folger is great for hunting out something specific, or for browsing: it's got everything from performance clips and academic lectures to discussions of theatre history and talks by leading Shakespearean actors.

Internet Shakespeare Editions
internetshakespeare.uvic.ca
Run by the University of Victoria in Canada, this is another treasure trove of performance history plus a selection of Shakespearean essays and critical work from all over the world.

The Shakespeare Birthplace Trust
shakespeare.org.uk
Not just a visit-Stratford site (although it's good for that, too), this incorporates a great Explore Shakespeare section, which has an unusually far-ranging selection of articles and blogs.

In print

Ackroyd, Peter, *Shakespeare: The Biography*, Vintage, 2006

Arnold, Katharine, *Globe: Life in Shakespeare's London*, Simon & Schuster, 2015

Bate, Jonathan, *The Genius of Shakespeare*, Picador, 2016

Bate, Jonathan, *Mad About Shakespeare: Life Lessons from the Bard*, William Collins, 2023

Bate, Jonathan, *Soul of the Age: The Life, Mind and World of William Shakespeare*, Penguin Books, 2009

Berry, Herbert, *Shakespeare's Playhouses*, AMS Press, 1987

Brigden, Susan, *New Worlds, Lost Worlds: The Rule of the Tudors, 1485–1603*, Penguin Books, 2001

Cowen Orlin, Lena, *The Private Life of William Shakespeare*, Oxford University Press, 2021

Duncan-Jones, Katherine, *Ungentle Shakespeare*, The Arden Shakespeare, 2001

Gurr, Andrew, *Playgoing in Shakespeare's London*, Cambridge University Press, 2009

Jones, Jeanne, *Family Life in Shakespeare's England: Stratford upon Avon, 1570–1630*, Sutton Publishing, 1996

Laoutaris, Chris, *Shakespeare's Book: The Intertwined Lives Behind the First Folio*, William Collins, 2023

Mortimer, Ian, *The Time Traveller's Guide to Elizabethan England*, Vintage, 2013

Pritchard, R. E. (ed), *Shakespeare's England: Life in Elizabethan & Jacobean Times*, Sutton Publishing, 2003

Shapiro, James, *1599: A Year in the Life of William Shakespeare*, Faber and Faber, 2005

Shapiro, James, *Contested Will: Who Wrote Shakespeare?* Faber and Faber, 2011

Wells, Stanley, *Shakespeare & Co.: Christopher Marlowe, Thomas Dekker, Ben Jonson, Thomas Middleton, John Fletcher and the Other Players in His Story*, Penguin Books, 2007

Wells, Stanley, *What Was Shakespeare Really Like?*, Cambridge University Press, 2023

Wood, Michael, *In Search of Shakespeare*, BBC Books, 2005

Index

Credits

The publisher would like to thank the following for permission to reproduce copyright material. All reasonable efforts have been made to trace copyright holders and to obtain their permission for the use of copyright material. The publisher apologises for any errors or omissions and will gratefully incorporate any corrections in future reprints if notified.

Alamy: 62, 128, 154, 155

Artvee: 21, 29 top, 92 left, 95, 103, 106, 113 right, 142 left, 147, 152

Creative Commons: 6, 10–11, 15 left, 17, 18 left, 20 right, 22, 23 right, 24, 26, 27 middle & bottom, 29 bottom, 30–31, 36, 38–39, 40 left & centre, 41–42, 43 right, 46, 49 top right & bottom, 51, 53 top, 54 right, 60, 64, 67, 71 left, 72 top, 77, 79 right, 80, 85 bottom, 94 left, 99–100, 104 left, 107 bottom, 108, 109 left, 118 bottom left, 119 left, 133, 153, 156 bottom

Europeana: 25 right

Flickr: 56, 75

Folger Shakespeare Library: 7 top, 28, 44, 50, 52, 55, 65 top, 66 right, 71 right, 73, 82 (left and centre), 84, 86, 88–90, 93 bottom, 102 left, 105 top, 109 right, 111, 113 left, 116, 119 right, 120, 122–23, 129, 131, 134, 136–37, 139, 140 right, 141 left, 148, 149 bottom

Getty Images: 3, 15 right, 23 left, 49 top left, 81 bottom, 141 right, 142 right, 144 right, 149 top

Hereford Cathedral: 73 bottom

Internet Archive: 9, 25 left, 37, 43 left, 117 left, 127, 151 bottom

ITOLDYA: 14 left

Jeni Kirby History: 117 right

Library of Congress: 14 right, 70, 98

Look and Learn History Picture Archive: 5, 7 bottom, 16, 33, 40 right, 45, 47 bottom, 53 bottom, 57, 61, 63, 65 bottom, 66 left, 74, 76 right, 78, 83, 85 top, 87, 92 right, 93 top, 101, 102 right, 104 right, 105 bottom, 114–15, 126, 130, 132 right, 140 left, 143, 144 left, 145–46, 150, 156 top left & top right

The Metropolitan Museum of Art: 8, 19, 138

New York Public Library: 79 left

Picryl: 32

Project Gutenberg: 27 top, 110

Public Domain Pictures: 58 top, 155 right

Raw Pixel: 118 top left

Shutterstock: 1, 18 right, 59 left, 112 right, 121 bottom, 132 left

Wellcome Collection: 20 left, 47 top, 54 left, 59 right, 76 left, 81 top, 94 right, 107 top, 112 left, 121 top, 135, 151 top

Yale Center for British Art: 58 bottom

Yale University Art Gallery: 91